PART I: STRIVING TO STAY WITH A GOD OF SURPRISES
PART II: STEPPING WILDLY INTO THEOLOGY

END OF DAYS?
REVISED EDITION

iUniverse books may be ordered through booksellers or by contacting:

iUniverse
1663 Liberty Drive
Bloomington, IN 47403
www.iuniverse.com
1-800-Authors (1-800-288-4677)

Because of the dynamic nature of the Internet, any web addresses or links contained in this book may have changed since publication and may no longer be valid. The views expressed in this work are solely those of the author and do not necessarily reflect the views of the publisher, and the publisher hereby disclaims any responsibility for them.

Any people depicted in stock imagery provided by Getty Images are models, and such images are being used for illustrative purposes only.
Certain stock imagery © Getty Images.

ISBN: 978-1-5320-5656-7 (sc)
ISBN: 978-1-5320-5657-4 (e)

Library of Congress Control Number: 2018910448

Print information available on the last page.

iUniverse rev. date: 09/14/2018

END OF DAYS?

Revised Edition

JOHN O. HUNTER

Table of Contents Part I

I

Introduction

I grew up in a different country. Pale impressions of it appear now and then, but complete changes in social and moral attitudes during my lifetime distinguish that country from the one I am living in now at the end of my time. I still value the friends I had when I was growing up in Niagara Falls, NY, and of course my family— the value which is never lost regardless of our mistakes. But the things I learned in the halcyon days of my youth are disappearing and old attitudes of respect for the bedrocks of our culture and society seem less prevalent, at least in political circles and I fear in academic circles as well.

As one of my poet friends said,

"Nothing can bring back the splendor in the grass." (William Wordsworth)

And another," A crowd will gather, and not know it walks the very street whereon a thing once walked that seemed a burning cloud." (WB Yeats)

How has it all happened? Or am I wrong? Is it I who am off course? "God is in his heaven and all is right with the world"?

But no, not for me, and I suspect the same for some of my older friends: How long does it take for the country to become utterly foreign? Who among us elders would have thought 40 years ago that the traditional idea of marriage could become emptied of meaning? that there would be a growing market for the body parts of aborted babies? or that the basic freedoms of speech and religion would come under attack?

40 years ago we still had primitive notions that the father of a child had some inescapable duty toward not only the baby but to the mother! that infanticide and suicide could never become legal! that no state or city or even the President of the United States could deny the rule of law!

Does the roaring current of change mean that our country as "an exceptional nation" will soon become incomprehensible to young people, knowing nothing of their roots? Will my country, recently vanished, leave enough connection to the principles of law and order and the ideal of justice to sustain their faith in e Plurabis Unum?

I have been an educator all my adult life. Now as I approach the end and survey the field of higher education where I was once productive and shared good results with my colleagues, I see waste and retreat and cowardice. I am reminded of Ozymandias:

"Nothing beside remains. Round the decay of that colossal wreck, boundless and bare, the lone and level sands stretch far away. " (Percy B. Shelley)

Maybe I am wrong, I hope so, but I do not see today the leadership, sense of purpose and commitment to standards of excellence that are essential to maintaining our place as a great and exemplary nation.

We were warned by George Orwell. It is not our constitutional form of government that signifies the problem: Rather it is government reticulated in an immense and growing bureaucracy that dulls effectiveness, leads to gridlock, and creates the condition for corruption and the spread of evil. The growth of bureaucracy makes it very difficult to revitalize our institutions.

I shall not continue with these lamentations because I still have hope for our young folks: Some of them are like the snowflakes on college campuses, and we worry about their sense of direction or lack thereof. But others are still winners and show wonderful traits. They are amazing athletes,some excell academically and are very smart and articulate, and they are not decieved. I don't know if these are the majority, but I shall be rooting for them.

For this Phoenix to rise, a new class of leaders must emerge to summon the courage and drive for a resurrection of basic Western values, and to contend with the surge of technological development that puts artificial intelligence front and center. In itself this will be an awesome challenge— as well as primary hope for the future if it is in God's absorbing light.

Nostalgia

Nostalgia, once considered a neurological disorder, may now be properly regarded as a driving force of poetry. When Humphrey Bogart says to Ingrid Bergman in *Casablanca,* "we'll always have Paris," that's nostalgia.

And so I embrace it in connection with some acquaintances of mine from long ago. Many years passed with no contact, but I have been blessed in these final days by memories and some reconnection, however oblique, with some kids I grew up with in the "project" of Griffon Manor in the City of Niagara Falls, NY, where I attended Niagara St. School and graduated from La Salle High School on Buffalo Ave. in 1950 when I was 16 years old.

These were some of my pals: Ron and Velzie Laughlin, Bill Corp, Tommy Webster, Jerry Tessier, Johnny Williams, Bill Ryan,Pete Eodice and the Garvey brothers, and my little buddy protege, Bobby Campbell. We formed teams and played sandlot baseball and tackle football— without equipment and thought nothiing of it. We did not have umpires or referees and it was never a problem. We joined the Boy Scouts Troop 11, and when we were 16 a few of us lied about our age and joined the Air National Guard at Niagara Falls Airport.

Ron and Velzie I saw for the last time in 2009 at the home of my sister, Jean, who liked to play cowboys with us. Ron was my best buddy in those dappled days of innocence when we crashed the woods of Cayuga Creek and threw spears at imaginary foes,learned to swim in the Little River (getting out once in a while to let garbage piles float by), learned to play basketball, with thanks to Norm in the project gym (how I loved that sport!),and went "cooning" for grapes, and played chicken on River Road, and went after led astray birds in North Tonawanda.

I was enthralled at the age of twelve to own a single shot 22 rifle. There was no marked traffic for handguns or assault rifles in those days, and violence in our schools was not a daily topic of conversation. I guess we did not know how blessed we were.

Bill Corp and Bill Ryan I have not seen since LaSalle High School on Buffalo Ave. Both became very successful; most of the project kids did very well. I do not recall any serious drug addiction in those days, but I guess alcoholism was a problem for some in later years. Somehow Bill and Bill and I found each other through internet magic in recent years, a minor touch but important because this reverie helps to amalgamate lifetime of experience.

I cannot think of lyrics more appropriate to mark such bittersweet rediscovery that happens to all of us than the universal anthem of Robert Burns:

> *Should auld acquaintance be forgot,*
> *And never brought to mind?*
> *Should auld acquaintance be forgot,*
> *And days o'auld lang syne?*
>
> *For auld lang syne, my dear*
> *For auld lang syne,*
> *We'll tak a cup o'kindness yet*
> *For auld lang syne!*
> *(old long ago)*

Yes, Nostalgia is great!

Elaine and John, Suzan and Becky

I want you to sit next to me on the edge of this little pond and see and hear all that we can — the rippling clean water, the murmur of hidden streams, the morning Robin and the shy Cardinal, the swirl of the fierce little sparrows, and the harsh voices as the curtain rises on a new day. Now we know how truly important it is to find time for solitary being and soft family.

Mother's Constant Refrain

"Tell me the tales that to me were so dear,
long, long ago, long, long ago,
sing me the songs I delighted to hear,
long, long ago, long ago."

Suzanne's Poem

A mother's hand shares that first earthly touch
the gift of life and more the gift of love.
For the child who reaches to grasp and clutch,
her hold so gentle in the care thereof,
there is raw power in maternal touch,
her stroke sets rhythm for the rest of time.
Today I am surely blessed so very much
because the aged hand which once held mine
was one of a pair that without applaud
did also choose to hold the hand of God.
                    (Suzanne Hunter)

II
Life Purpose/Meaning

According to our Declaration of Independence, which is surely the most inspirational political document ever written, the pursuit of happiness is an integral part of the American Dream.

But I ask you to think about it: Can happiness really be pursued?

Victor Frankl, the Holocaust survivor and founder of logotherapy, thinks not: "Happiness cannot be pursued, it must ensue." In other words, you must have a reason to be happy, and that reason begins with purpose that gives meaning to your life.

I thank God that I have never chased money, yet more than enough has come to me. I think it's true that in our materialistic society, we are too accustomed to measuring our value in money. The idea of materialistic gain has put a hole in many hearts.

I believe that the best use of a life is "to spend it for something that outlasts it." In order to do that you need meaningful relationships that matter. For me it is not my achievements that mattered so much as the people relationships in those achievements and the meaning in those relationships that satisfied or dissatisfied me. I want to be loyal to those people who gave meaning to my life, even when I can see the times when they did not return my loyalty, sadly to admit.

Have you noticed that when you wake up to something you really want to do, you are pleased and you look forward to it? It's because you have a purpose, and the purpose gives meaning to your life. Then you can think about the quality of your life.

I believe this is truth, but it took me a long time to learn it. In my early years it was just my ego pushing my desire to achieve or win something. I can no longer attend to the goals I once had, but my life still has meaning. I find that meaning in "writing myself clear" as well as in fulfilling obligations, some of which I would rather not have.

When there is meaning in our lives the door is open for *commitment*. Deeply held commitment to a noble objective will win every time. Angels come forth to help, instruments and events completely unanticipated to make the difference between failure and success even if the failure seemed impossible to shake.

A meaningful life is marked by purposeful choices that will not always make you happy but may give you something vastly more important to dwell upon— the possibility of God's grace.

When I was a teenager I wanted to be a star basketball player but that was just a fantasy. Later, after some years of confusion, I wanted to be a good teacher and then I began to come into my true purpose. Still I did not have a strong philosophic or values ground for myself.

Let's be clear, however, that the quality of a purposeful life may not be enrolled with goodness. The world's most brutal dictators, evil to the core of their being, had strong purpose. Hitler is the most obvious example in his determination to annihilate the Jewish population. Stalin and Mao Zedung had comparable motivations. So it is indeed important to evaluate a leader's purpose.

Humankind has always engaged in a dialectical process— the struggle of good and evil— and the good guys do not always win. But yes, there are some absolutes.

It was not until I began to contemplate Christian experience— Thomas Merton, Alexander Solzhenitsyn, John Paul II were big for me— that I found a spiritual connection for my evaluation. My conversion path has been long but God has been good to me.

I make no claims to ultimate victories. I am still plodding along, but now at least I know that reconciliation is possible. Christ does not leave us to face our trials alone.

I'm persuaded that most people do not have a well thought out values framework. Some do not even want to think about this stuff; they just want to live their lives unbothered. My contrary thought does not make me superior in any way, but I believe this topic is worthy of reflection, especially for young people whose minds are naturally attracted to the essence of life until it is all flattened out.

Something happened in the last century dangerous to the souls of young people: the triumph of the tyranny of ideological conviction, especially political correctness and moral relativism. These are a savage blight on their education and budding sense of purpose.

I leave this writing primarily for them and of course for my family. With this leave I also submit these prayers:

Thank you Lord for blessing my life and the lives of my children. Thank you for showing me goodness and beauty in the world, the lyrical foundation of things. Thank you for your healing power, your lovingkindness and your forgiveness. Thank you for being the light of our world, the Alpha and the Omega.

Also I submit this thanksgiving blessing from our Native American brothers and sisters: *Great father, send us your breath over the lakes, hills and prairies, that our world may be beautiful and peaceful for our children, and our people strong.*

III

Our Land Betrayal

In my 2012 book, *Chasing Crazy Horse: A Wasichu Interpretation of the Lakota Tragedy,* I traced the tragedy of the great Lakota (Sioux) nation which took the brunt of the despoliation and devastation of High Plains country in the 19th century. At the beginning of the century there were 50 million Buffalo roaming the plains. The Prairie, estimated to cover 700,000 square miles of native grasslands, encompassed an area comparable in size and majesty to the Gulf of Mexico— a cornucopia of wildlife and flora sensationally rich and beautiful. More than 40% of the country was once open Prairie, grassland that extended from Missouri to Montana. This was the natural condition of the land. Water from meandering streams and lakes and rivers was clean, plentiful and free, and constantly replenishing deep sweetwater aquifers. "God shed His grace on thee."

What was chosen to be done in order to build a new nation included removal of the Indians and the Buffalo and along the way the destruction of the Prairie.

The deeply rooted Prairie grasses were replaced by farmland and pasture land maintained by pesticide and herbicide poisons. It was not long before the "war on roots" swept the rich black soil away and set the stage for a vast dustbowl. In Iowa today there are Prairie relicts, not many, but a few the locals call "postage stamp prairies." Some stand as islands in an unbroken sea of farm land. From some of these relicts, all once level with the surrounding flatland, one must step down three feet or so to walk from Prairie on to plowed land. The force that bound this wealth together was roots that went to depths of 10 feet or more, compared to replacement foreign grasses introduced of a mere six to nine inches.

The goal of settlement of the West was to bring land under the plow according to the great dream of creating independent communities— in place of the nomadic Indian camps that revered the land the way it was— and establishing agriculture as the way of life. Thus America was made prosperous. And the skies were not cloudy all day.

But no! it was not easily accomplished! Life on the Western frontier was hard and dangerous. It required men and women of exceptional character—tough, resilient, honest, able to face life squarely, without excuse for failure, and with pride in what they were creating. A frontier ethic was born and became ingrained in the American conscience. Truly, a dialectic was at work pitting the values of individuality and free enterprise against the wealth, beauty and spirit of nature. The founders of the American dream believed in the fundamental importance of hard work and good character as noble in itself and essential to human flourishing.

The hard left ideological critique that these entrepreneurial Americans were guilty of lawless, unremitting exploitation of the land and natural resources, leaving nothing to redeem their aggression, is a wildly overdrawn argument. For all the sins committed, most of the folks who settled the American frontier were simply trying to find their place.

But their intrepid and essentially decent nature did not extend to their natural brothers, the American Indians, who were already on the land before them. The moral vision of the time was tragically constrained. The forces of conflict were not diabolical, but they were deep and dirty and unforgiving on all sides.

Could it all have been done differently in ways that would have synthesized and harmonized the best common values and preserved our natural wealth? Yes, we can see that now in the aftermath, and perhaps there is some salvation through restoration efforts of sterling organizations such as *Earthjustice, Natural Resources Defense Council, National Wildlife Federation, Audubon, Nature Conservancy, and Sierra Club.*

IV
The Power of Propaganda

The differences of pure art and propaganda art are exemplified many ways and times in popular writings. Two examples of powerful propaganda art are Karl Marx and Friedrich Engels' *The Communist Manifesto*, and Harriet Beecher Stowe's *Uncle Tom's Cabin*.

No question they both had enormous appeal and influence. Marx still has appeal in academic circles, but the systems he helped to spawn through communist ideology are now in the "ash heap of history." No communist revolution was brought off in the Marxist way, and his prophecy of the "withering away of the state" was always absurd.

Stowe's work is a somewhat different case. If there is such a thing as a great propaganda art, *Uncle Tom's Cabin* is it, but it does not tell the true story of slavery in the South. (A more reliable account is Nathalie Dessins', *Myths of the Slave Plantation*, 2003, or see WJ Cash, *The Mind of the South*, 1941.

Following her quick climb to celebrity status, Stowe was invited to visit the Scottish Highlands at the time of the "Clearances". While seeing more of Scotland than she did of Kentucky, she was unwittingly suborned by the Scottish aristocracy and became an accomplice in an evil on par with slavery. She wrote *Sunny Memories* as an account of her visit. Her utter naïveté and blindness to the terrible cruelties afflicted on the Highlanders at the hands of their own clan chiefs— certainly as bad or worse than southern slave masters— is graphically captured in John Prebble's *The Highland Clearances*,1963.

As we sometimes say of people we like, "Mrs. Stowe had a good heart and her righteousness was worthy." But she had no talent for finding the truth. It is astonishing to realize that her single work is still considered by some college faculty as great literature, as I discovered in a conversation that rated *Uncle Tom's Cabin* as a greater novel than Herman Melville's *Moby Dick*.

Ephemeral though it may be, propaganda is sometimes compelling indeed! In today's mass media and information systems it is a constant ferocious driver of public and self deception. The ideologies of cultural relativism and religious fanaticism often combine with propaganda to create further confusion and threaten chaos in the public realm.

Many journalists, politicians, and even educators do not understand or respect the normative values of personal integrity and dignity endowed by our Creator on all human beings. Mistaken conclusions about people's incapacity to discern truth are constantly made based on observations of intolerance and incivility. Historically, these have always been problems in democratic society, due in part to the freedom, missing in totalitarian regimes, given to propagandists and demagogues. But it is wrong to generalize from remarks of a bunch of rancorous or even malevolent individuals who have momentarily seized the spotlight.

When the individual citizen is left free to judge and to choose without fear of consequences, relying on his/her natural intelligence, the distinctions can be made between advocacy and analysis in the information presented. This may not always be the case, but mere propaganda need not win. It is an elitist mistake to underestimate the average person's intelligence.

We live in an ideological age that forges denial of the human soul's connection to truth and goodness. For many people it is still too much to grasp that there is an immutable moral law. Yet, for most people, even under the cynical weight of collective propaganda, a principled point of view is not beyond call.

Does not "good propaganda" have a positive effect? Possibly so, if it ripples the flow of action to good ends. But propaganda plays on the surface of things. It lacks the depth and authenticity of quest for truth— truth that through time will make a universal claim. So it was that despite their false doctrine of lies and propaganda, even harnessed to great political and literary power, Hitler's

Third Reich, the Bolsheviks and the Soviet Union, Apartheid, and Saddam Hussein's Iraq, all fell in the short span of the 20ᵗʰ century.

And so we may believe in John Milton's *Areopagitica*:

"Though all the winds of doctrine were let loose to play upon the earth, so Truth be in the field, we do injuriously by licensing and prohibiting to doubt her strengths: let Truth and falsehood grapple; whoever knew Truth put to worse in a free and open encounter."

Notes on War on Women

Theodore Dalrymple, a brilliant psychiatrist (somewhat in the mold of Charles Krauthammer) tells the story of a young Muslim woman who wanted to go to work and live like a Western woman. In the eyes of her parents and brothers there could be no worse insult to the family, but eventually they gave way because they needed the money.

So this young woman who had been subdued all of her life went to work and in doing so found freedom. She loved her work which was a daily release from prison at home, the only time she was allowed out. The work was like air after suffocation. When I was president, I would have been glad to hire her and otherwise oppressed Muslim women to work for me. But that was not the attitude of her brothers who wanted westernized lives for themselves but not for their sisters. This may be explainable in a Muslim culture which does not value the autonomy and individuality of their women.

But what explains the attitude of our feminists who subscribe to the "war on women"? In our colleges and universities especially we see and hear them fearlessly fighting for speech codes and politically correct language (should we say "personhole" rather than "manhole cover"?) while their veiled sisters in the middle east continue to suffer oppression and physical abuse, including torture, and nary a word do we hear about it.

But of course we do know: it's all about ideology.

V

Flashpoints and Endpoints

"Despair is only for those who see the end beyond all doubt." (J.R.R. Tolkien)

Elsewhere I have argued the difference between physical evolution and spiritual evolution and the hope for a new ground being formed which authentically combines science and faith through the collaboration of human beings and super intelligent machines, coming soon in the invention of a brave new world. This will be the next flashpoint of evolution and the ultimate challenge of the next generation. If God is left out of the equation, the outcome will be *apocalyptic extremis*— with a bang or a whimper it won't matter— truly the End of Days.

My friends and I will not face it, but my grandchildren might. I wish that we could be of more support for them. I can only hope that genes of courage and integrity have passed on to them, and that they will bond with other like souls.

Let me enter a word of humility here: My current view is that nobody really knows anything. To accurately predict the future is an unreasonable quest, especially so for technological forecasting, but as the monks of Genesee Abbey know, our God is a God of love and sometimes, a God of surprises.

Of all the institutional damages we have experienced in my lifetime, I grieve most the killing of "the liberal arts tradition." in our colleges and universities. I would not recommend for any

potential student what is left of this once supremely valuable program. I say this with gratitude for my own liberal arts matriculation many years ago in the hands of admirable professors.

One introduced me to literary criticism, another to the Socratic method — both aimed at search for the truth — and a third to history of civilization (which he sometimes taught in Latin.) Others sressed the connection of good writing and logic. There was no fierce political indoctrination such as we have today! I liked and trusted all of my teachers.

These "scholars and gentlemen/ladies" could move a circle of students to ardent discussion of factual knowledge, and very importantly, issues and value differences, without rancor or hyperbole— or at least, if these distractions came up, would try to restore the circle's integrity. By no means did they seek conformity of opinion. While I was not an all star student in those days, almost inadvertently I discovered something magnificent that set me on a course eventually to become my professional life. It is a process of rational inquiry and dialectical arrival at conclusions.

Keep three skills in balance: Inquiry, Acknowledgment, Advocacy. There is truth to be found but none of us will ever have sole possession of it. You never know what you don't know.

We see the world from our own perspectives. Each of us has our own story. Learning someone else's story or side of the issue may let us see something we didn't see before. In this learning conversation we ask questions about the information— examine the empirical data— trace our interpretations of it.

The process goal is always the same: what is the truth? Not what is most popular— or what is easiest to accept— or what or who will win an election?

Socrates stressed humility in the face of truth, but there is also room for enthusiasm! In fact, without it you can't get very far. The method does not rob you of your advocacy but it will test your assumptions and interpretations, strengthening or refining or amending them, helping you to clarify your position. The conversation ends with acknowledgment that there may still be something missing, something more to learn. At the same time if we are responsible for making a decision, we do not shrink from the responsibility. Rather we trust in our informed judgment.

Tough, honest criticism is essential, but throughout the process there is respect for the other guy or gal. It's demonstrated by acknowledging each other's position. To acknowledge of course is not the same thing as to agree. We may achieve a synthesis, or it may be that we simply agree to disagree, at least for the present. Without mutual understanding of the process it will simply stop. Embarrassed, friendly adversaries withdraw to the protection of banality; others may resort to violence.

In my youthful naïveté, it did not occur to me that such a beautiful approach could be undermined by our culture or threatened by another culture of death. Now there is something happening in our culture as it interacts with fantastic ideology which is threatening the process of rational inquiry and coarsening the dialogue.

Within our presumed democratic society, the decline of rational method and the resulting instability is traceable to both political excess and cultural fascination with image making and entertainment in which image is more important than truth.

We are bombarded mercilessly by images of all kinds, but the significant force is the image bending, the manipulation, distortion, even lies by professional media handlers and politicians who are very skilled and clever. They can turn the world upside down, building a mountain of irrationality— an Orwellian world— in which we are also witnessing a clash of civilizations.

Evils of the 20th century continued and exploded in the 21st with a significant twist: Much of the evil done now is freely chosen and not even characterized as such. I do not contend that government is the monster, but neither is government blameless for what now afflicts every country and has brought pain and suffering to its high peak.

It began with ideologies propounded by intellectuals, especially the idea that man/woman should be freed from the shackles of social convention and self-control. Anything goes. Our governments in the West responded by enacting laws that promoted unrestrained behavior and created welfare systems that protect people from their personal decisions.

There was a time, I can remember it, when chivalry would not sanction torture of women and children; transgressors were branded as cowards; the despots who fostered it would eminently deny their actions. Now, torture of the worst kind against innocents is standard practice with some governments and freely admitted, even boasted about.

Why do we have this rising tide of cruelty and joyous malignity that staggers but does not appease human imagination for inhumanity? Is it the poverty? No that is the biggest canard! In a time of much less prosperity not so long ago, such conduct was much less widespread; the evil was contained to evil men.

Metaphorically speaking, it may be seen as a legacy of Original Sin. Contemporaneously, it is better explained as far ranging moral cowardice, justified because we know now that everyone is entitled to their own opinion and their own way of life. In the decline of the West there is no scale of human values as there once was. The winning argument on the international scene is moral equivalence.

Though I now observe from the outside, the evidence suggests that some of today's professors, not all but too many, are more interested in particular ideologies than they are in objective scholarship and balanced search for the truth and justice. What happened?

How did the current orientation to ideology become so strong that many of these "educators" do not even know they are caught in an ideological trap?) I suspect that Schools of Education and "student development" staff members have a lot to do with it. I saw it first, taken by surprise, in England in the mid-1980s when scandalous means to control who would be allowed to speak in public forums and lectures emerged. Essentially unchallenged, this fascism metastasized and is now rampant in American as well as British universities.

I did not experience it in Alfred in the 80s, and there may still be other small colleges which hold on to the traditional values of academe, but I fear that many of our colleges and universities have lost their way. Too many college administrations are feckless in dealing with assaults on campus freedom and institutional integrity.

I do not know how true this is of our grade schools. I have two daughters who teach in elementary school and are committed to their students and do not share my trepidation. I was amazed when a small group of the students from a poor environment eagerly accepted a gift of classic books. I am glad for these tokens, so I want to be cautious here, but we need to acknowledge some serious problems that interfere drastically with student growth and development today, including a wretched drug culture our kids face that exceeds anything we knew in my youth.

Heroin is cheaper than many painkillers and is easily accessible even in small NY towns like Hornell and Canaseraga, a phenomenon unknown in the Griffin Manor housing project where I grew up.

Big Pharma rules: America is now a fully loaded drug addiction society beginning with drugs prescribed every day at pharmacies, used/abused at hospitals, and introduced to children at an early age (Ritalin). Parents and counselors are astonished to realize how quickly the addiction can happen. A teenager may be neck-deep in drug addiction and completely unable to break away on his/her own.

Equally troublesome (and scary) is emphasis on social media: Have you ever watched a bunch of teen-agers sitting on a couch but not bothering to converse with each other, too absorbed in listening to a cell-phone connection? — portent of a superficial plasticised existence?

VI
Love of Truth

We know that we live in a material world which compels us to stay with rational interpretations and logical discovery— the scientific method. Angels around us, faeries living with us, visions of an alternative existence, parallel universes— these notions are easily dispelled even though we frequently find them on our entertainment channels. They continue to have credence. Actually they have been in our minds for a long time, longer than the age of science.

So how do we know the truth of anything? Some philosophers tell us that the truth is totally subjective: We do not live in the world, we live in a picture or vision of it that we have formed. Others say that truth is external and objective. On the extreme end is the "true believer" who not only knows that he has the whole truth but is responsible to see that others accept it also.

But the lover of truth I believe is somewhere in between: He or she comes to recognize that the truth of anything is measured slowly, yet the desire for it is universal.

The lover of truth does not confuse sincerity or passion with truth. He or she is aware that it is easy to be deceived, especially by ourselves. The search is not easy. Lies and bad faith may not always appear as such; they may wear the mask of truth.

Truth is aive; it grows and deepens as a person develops. What was true at 20 may have new meaning at 50. Truth is not just an accumulation of "facts" though these may be essential in the discovery process. I find companions for truth in poets such as WB Yeats and Robert Burns; in saints such as Patrick and John Paul; and in forgotten American leaders such as Crazy Horse and Chief Joseph. They break through conventional worldviews.

When I was growing up my teachers sought to put me on the right track by demythologizing or "debunking" everything. I learned that anything mythical was false, unreal, unhistorical or unscientific. A "myth" corresponded to a lie. I realize now what a disservice it was to me personally when I bought into this crimped way of looking at the world. To impart culture as though history is what happened and myth is fiction distorts our understanding of who we are and where we come from.

I see how powerful the myth is and how essentially true and fundamental to a coherent, sane explanation of reality it may be. In America we share many myths which shape our sense of national consciousness and even our destiny.

One of the most prevalent is the "American Dream."

Usually it means the chance for a better life in America, upward mobility, the opportunity to succeed through hard work, "pulling us up by our own bootstraps," the idea of reinventing oneself, living in a land of law and order. In the past two decades, this myth has been downplayed.

Some faculty go out of their normal curriculum to dispel the myth of the American Dream. They want a different ideological orientation that often seems to translate to "Hate America" stuff.

I believe this attitude is a cancer not only on the spirit of America but on the institutions which hold her up and focus on the important work of trying to solve long term problems, including the racial divide. America is not a racist nation: We could not have elected a black president if that were true, but it would be foolish to say that we do not have serious racial issues. Rightly understood and fostered, the American Dream could be used as an effective cultural tool in the struggle for *e Pluribus Unum.* For a long time it has been but now seems to be threatened by other emerging ideological myths, such as "Black Lives Matter."

Mistaken ideology by some college presidents and their student life administrators, that students should be worried about language that might violate campus rules or " hurt the feelings"of other students is a harbinger for violent censorship and a platform for continuing mob attacks. If today's authorities continue to foster the notion that silencing opponents is what good people do, the time is coming when dissenters on college campus will be beaten and even murdered. The ideologies of moral authoritarianism and identity politics will replace our once dearly embraced ideals of liberty and justice, and even well-intentioned radicals will not understand the wreckage they have wrought, or know what has happened to their institutions.

VII

God's Evidence (and St.Patrick)

Immanuel Kant, the foremost Enlightenment philosopher, said that the existence of God can neither be proven nor disproven. In philosophical terms that may be so,but as a practical proposition there is abundant evidence of His presence in humankind's moral consciousness, which therefore keeps developing.

Ego baptizo te in nomine Patris et filio et spiritus sancti.

Tibi gratias ago pro tui Domine sanitatem potentiae, mansuetudinem tuam, et dimittetur ei.

I begin by using Latin, not to claim fluency (I am not). I use it to espouse my claim to Christian heritage through an old language, much older than modern English, Latin conveys the deep strength of ancient, universal (catholic) authority, exemplified through the Eucharist or Lord's Supper, celebrated in many forms throughout the centuries of Christianity.

It penetrates to an even more ancient glorification of what endures through time, revealed in the ceremonial practices of Greco-Roman culture, Mongolian culture in the time of Genghis Khan,hence its translation to Chinese civilization, and ultimately in our own.

What endures? what is everlasting? comes down through the ages as a revenant transaction of God's power through humankind? — scriptures, an event memorialized, a work of art, a Place, hollowed ground,sacred mountains, words of an unchallenged tradition — all of these wondrous deposits exceedingly more powerful than current false- profound philosophies and doctrines that erode our capacity for understanding His truth.

In this time of blazing uncertainty, we need to know the absoluteness of God's presence and grace by reaching for those signs and artifacts of it through the ages — enforced also by knowledge of those leaders embraced by God,destined to perform great works regardless of accidental religious persuasion,who possessed an instinctoid awareness of human needs:Founders of Christianity Jesus and Paul, Patrick and other lesser lights,but still bright ; 5th / 6th Centuries BC Enlightenment of Siddhartha Gautama (The Buddha) and Confucious, China's most famous philosopher and teacher.

And Genghis Khan,known for his bloody conquests but a truly remarkable leader who built the largest land empire in world history, liberated the people of the steppes and gave them rule by law and national dignity.These Steppe Mongols were hardly barbarians;they were among the most enlightened people on earth.

Also interesting to note, in the mid-13th Century. this vast Mongolian empire,including China still being conquered, was managed by Mongol women who declared themselves as Christians at a time when Mongolian official policy was religious freedom. The Khan used his daughters as rulers of his domains because he saw their natural talents for governing as superior to the potential of his sons. Thus, almost 1000 years before us, women's rights were proclaimed. (Family note: this was same time Hunterstone was being built in Scotland.)

Yes, there is a lot of paradox in human accomplishment.

Following Jesus and Paul, Patrick is our man.

Saint Patrick

I rise today through a mighty strength, the invocation of the Trinity.(St.Patrick'sLorica)

Life gives to each of us a mix of pleasure and regret.Of all the things I am proud of in this life one on the top shelf is that my mother gave birth to me on St. Patrick's Day.

Revered as the patron saint of the Irish, Patrick was not Irish.

His birthplace and year of birth are not exactly known, but he was born somewhere on the west coast of Great Britain about 400 A.D. in what is now called Scotland or Wales. His family was well-to-do.

At the age of 16 he was kidnapped by some Irish pirates and sold into slavery in Ireland. He served as a slave for six years, tending sheep herds for his master. His life as a shepherd was endless misery. Left alone with the sheep in the hills, he was usually cold, hungry to the point of starvation,without shelter, and forlorn.

But this was also a time when his soul surged: he went deep into his inner self to gain spiritual command. He realized that there was more to this beautiful land with its lush green hills where he had been placed and more intended for him than what he was doing.

At that time his name was Maewyn Succat. It was later changed to Patrick when Pope Celestine canonized Maewyn to sainthood.

Did he drive out the snakes in Ireland? The factual answer is no, there were never any snakes in Ireland; but there is also a spiritual answer. While on his green hillside with the sheep, he began to think that he was not a good person and would go to hell when he died. In this quiet time of misery and sorrow Maewyn reached out and found his Lord, Jesus Christ.

Then by God's grace he was able to escape and return to his earlier home, but there was no intention by God or Maewyn for him to stay there. He had fallen in love with Ireland, and after a visit to Rome, returned to his adopted country as a missionary to proclaim the gospel of Jesus Christ.

He is celebrated and honored on March 17 for bringing the light of Jesus Christ to the people he loved.

Until the advent of Christianity, the common religious beliefs were that of paganism and druidism, full of fear, terror and captivity of darkness. By bringing the light of Christianity into Ireland, he drove out the "snakes of evil." In less than a century the Irish Catholic Church, as distinct from Roman though allegient to the Pope, was founded.

Patrick used three leaf clovers of the Shamrock to explain to his people the three persons of the Godhead – Father, Son and Holy Spirit – Blessed Holy Trinity that we confess in Patrick's Prayer of Lorica. He taught that it is not our physical death we should fear but our spiritual death, being totally separated from God. Thus he restored us, as Jesus and his disciples did, to hope, faith and love.

And so I say to my family and friends, HAPPY SAINT PATRICK'S DAY!

It took me a long time to learn this, and I almost missed it.

JOH: March 17, 2015

Postscript: I discovered the facts of this story when I visited the island of Iona, just off Craigmure, Scotland several years ago. I still remember this experience vividly: the monastery and nave where I found information on the lives of St. Patrick and St. Columba, the huge Celtic crosses, long hours spent on the rocky cliffs above the harbor, the charm of a little house where I stayed at Craigmure, and the walk across the moor to the ferry. I only regret that I did not return.

VIII

Mythology and Victimology The Orestian Myth

We know from recent advances in our study of different cultures, and thanks to leading thinkers such as Carl Jung that a myth persists — that is, it is a myth— precisely because it is true. The same myths are found in culture after culture throughout the ages.

I don't mean to say that they are literally true— there is a good deal of symbolism involved with myths— but they are true in what they tell us about human nature and the human condition. We may find a truth about ourselves in a myth;sometimes,we must dig to find that truth, but the digging is worthwhile.

Of course, it's important to be able to recognize a myth. There are big differences between the myth and a fairytale. For example, Santa Claus, who has been around only for a couple hundred years, is just a fairytale. Likable though he may be, he will never make it to the status of myth.

In his book, <u>The Road Less Traveled</u>, M. Scott Peck uses the myth of Orestes to discuss healthy personality. This is another of the myths associated with the Trojan Wars in ancient Greece.

As Peck explains, Orestes was a young man caught in a great moral dilemma when he discovered that his mother had murdered his father. The greatest obligation that a young Greek boy had was to avenge the murder of his father. On the other hand, the worst imaginable thing that he could do was to kill his mother. Following up on his obligation to avenge his father Orestes did kill his mother. Of course he had to pay a terrible price.

Pursued relentlessly by the Furies who would not let him escape from bad dreams and hallucinations, he was in continual torment until finally he prayed to the gods that they have mercy and release him. The gods held a trial for Orestes, and the Sun God, Apollo, represented him.

Apollo presented a defense that we hear used a lot today. Apollo said that what Orestes had done was not really his fault. Orestes, he said, had been placed in a terrible situation not of his choosing; he was a victim of circumstance and should not be held responsible.

Then something splendid and sensational happened: Orestes stood up and rejected Apollo's defense. No, he said, the truth is that I am responsible and I must bear the consequences.

The gods were amazed. This was the first time a mere mortal had accepted responsibility for his own actions, and the gods, who are used to being blamed for everything, decided to free him.

But there is even more. Orestes was not just restored. The Furies who had been persecuting him were replaced by three angels who were bearers of "grace and light." From out of the torment and sickness unto death, Orestes was brought to extraordinary health and wisdom.

IX

Genghis Khan and Crazy Horse

Of the world's warrior chiefs, the two most fascinating for me are Genghis Khan and the Lakota Crazy Horse, the latter far less notable, but they were similar in character and style:

Neither would allow an image/picture to be taken of him; both were fierce and fearless in command, yet humble in personal relations; both were innovative in their battle tactics and strategically brilliant; both were hated but respected by their enemies, and enormously loved by their tribe; both were secretly buried and burial site never revealed; both were excellent horsemen and loved horses (Crazy Horse at great risk went back on the battlefield to rescue one of his); Crazy Horse was reviled as a savage; the Khan in history has been compared, falsely, to Napolean and Hitler.

Both leaders saw beyond their physical lives. Genghis Khan was born of humble beginnings but became the mightiest conqueror the world has known, yet he did not seek to rule the world, his vision was "to end slavery and unite all peoples in peace under the <u>eternal blue skies."</u>

In the end, Crazy Horse was not successful. It is most likely that he knew in his heart that at least in this circle of life the Great Spirit would not save his people, yet he displayed a relentless fortitude.

That wonderful writer, Larry McMurtry, speculated that, even though Crazy Horse was "a man of charity and a living weapon and in his day was a kind of an eagle... he never made the kind of hardheaded assessment"... that came easily to the Khan.

Their stories differ in their deaths: Crazy Horse was betrayed and murdered, Genghis Kahn lived to old age and died surrounded by his loving family; his "spirit banner" was carried by Mongols for 800 years until destroyed in the totalitarian 20th Century. The biggest monument in the U.S. is built for Crazy Horse in Dakota plains territory "where his dead lie buried."

X

Vandals, Desperadoes, and Heroes

Did you ever think you would see what is now happening on our college campuses?— masked radicals punching women in the stomach? spitting and throwing feces? campus police asked to stand down while radicals vandalize buildings, set fire to classrooms, wreck automobiles, break windows?

Granted, many of the violaters are professional agitators, rather than students, all the more reason to enforce the law on campus. Time for BMOCS and WMOCS to intervene, college heroes, get up and get to it in a brave and orderly way. The vandals and desperadoes do not own the college!

Worst of all is that some college administrators simply stand aside ; some will even defend the chaos.

Who are these guys? not just the agitators but the administrators, who seem to be so weak and indecisive — not all, but enough of them to ask, "what do you think you're doing?" Are they just flying on the wings of ideology?

Hey, colleagues of mine, those who remember how optimistic we were about academic life 40 to 50 years ago: You may agree that the erosion of academic freedom and free speech on our college campuses today, obviously spreading, is the major threat to higher education, and perhaps to America as a whole.

In the 1960s, when young guys like me first entered into the arena, we still had the historical examples of what I consider to be the royalty of higher education, Harvard's Charles W. Elliott, Chicago's Robert M. Hutchins, Samuel P. Capen, University of Buffalo, and other presidents and professors who spoke with a strong sense of values, spiritual as well as intellectual.

Then the inspiration of Jacques Barzun, the premier model of a scholar and gentleman! (His book, <u>*Teacher in America, put me on solid ground in my first year of teaching, I am forever grateful.*</u>) Most of my professors seemed to be of that mold. Students of my generation who became my colleagues saw a field of promise that streched out for our years ahead.

What happened? Why were these rocks pushed aside? When I became president, I began to see the decline of liberal arts tradition and objective scholarship. There was a steady rise of the "isms"– – Marxism(even in English classrooms), Feminism, Freudianism, Deconstructionism – – cascading and running over the historic values of the pursuit of knowledge – – beauty, truth, the good! It began to seem that these purposes of liberal learning were shoved into a category of hopeless naïveté. They were also being jammed by political correctness and cultural relativism, now today claiming supremacy.

Where are the college presidents who should be defending academic values and upholding the law?. Whoever and wherever they are, I don't hear much about them. Too often, what is coming across to the public is weakness,lewdness, denigration of our Constitution, and ridicule of historical achievements— a stream of invective and hyperbole that so far seems to go on without challenge except for a few courageous organizations, such *as National Association of Scholars(NAS), American Council of Trustees and Alumni (ACTA), FIRE, Young Americans for Freedom(YAF), Academic Leadership Council.*Thank God for them and their allies.

Here I want to single out a few of the top organizations:Do we need leaders who will continue to distinguish First Amendment ideas from new options promoted for thought control? Do we need objective monitoring of blatant attempts to coerce students' political persuasion and affiliation? This is the mission and role of the NAS, as well as ACTA and YAF, aimed at focusing on the accountability of some of the major universities in our land.

The young people and seniors in these organizations are the true warriors and patriots, defending not only higher education but America as a whole in a time of national crisis.

What's behind all of the chaos? I believe it stems mainly from the Marxist orientation of radical left-wing professors who are striving to capture a "progressive" high ground for revolution that seeks to purge historic liberal balance, an "alienation of the intellectuals" that the eminent historian, Crane Brinton, posited as the first stage of revolution in his classic work, *Anatomy of Revolution.*

Why are there so few cool-headed folks on the academic front lines now? What happened to the old balanced engagement of "I disagree with you, but I will contend for your right to be wrong - - let's go get a beer and try to work it out."

Let's be clear and honest about it:There is a serious problem of teacher incompetency in secondary and post-secondary education, and an even greater problem of too many staff assistants who do not contribute to an educational mission. The resources spent there would be better used for the purpose of teaching kids at least to write a complete sentence.

The fault lies with Boards and administrations that were not alert to an Orwellian invasion,wrought primarily by Dewey- soaked schools of education and state agencies, but aided and abetted by our own lack of courage to stand up to assaults on institutional integrity and academic standards.

Yet somehow I do not feel despair: We are facing a crisis,but I remain confident that there is a residual cadre of committed professionals in education who could right the ship if they would step up to answer the call for meaningful reform.

As for the progressives,not all radical thinkers are deluded or to blame for the extremism of their colleagues. But it seems to me that too much of the language and action now unfolding is putting us on a slippery slope. Too many of our students and some of their professors are opting for violence, and so I worry more than I did before.

In my view, a lot of the dissonance is due to the media complex that loves to stir things up for ratings. What happened to the old professional journalism that tried to be impartial and thus helped us in a search for the truth? Has it been sunk by ideological warfare? Can we recover from the polarization and enjoy once again the honor and thrill of an objective teaching-learning process? I am confident that what we have seen in recent years is not a long-term trend. I believe that we can and shall recover from the progressive insurrection.

In my 50 years of mixing with college faculties,a few were knotheads, and may have claimed progressive identity, but the majority I knew were astute professors and teachers, truly committed to their students and their institution,competent in their disciplines, and good citizens. It's not possible that we have lost them all, but it's obvious that we need new leadership.

Some of that leadership will come in reminders of our personal autonomy and moral identity from new professors on the scene, such as Jordan Peterson of Toronto University. He sets a new tone, and others will follow.

XI
Leadership and Accountability

When I was College President, I was always talking about the "OD approach." I don't know how much of it survived me. In retrospect, I wonder how many of my listeners asked themselves, what's he talking about? OD? overdose? overdrive? I recall a humorous report back following presentation of the Blake and Mouton managerial grid, asking that we all strive to be 9/9 administrators. Does he mean that we should all work 9 to 9?

I think I did get through eventually, but there was nothing fancy about it. It's a matter of demanding competency and integrity, both personal and professional,and a willingness to be accountable.

From what I observe today, college presidents are managers, not leaders. They strive to survive and are too subservient to the political expectations of their faculty.

As a leader, the president, and other leading administrators,must lay down some basic principles and concepts that establish a values framework for the organization.

*The U.S.Constitution and Bill of Rights are highly respected documeents on this campus and wil be followed (let them argue about it but do not compromise.)

*Ensure that only well qualified faculty and staff will be appointed.

*A student is not an interruption of our work: he/she is the purpose of it.

*Don't complicate the teaching process, back it up! Simplify and streamline procedures as much as possible.

*Expect integrity in all relationships; when reporting a mistake tell the whole truth of it; above all, don't tolerate dishonesty or lies.

*Don't rely on memos to solve problems, and don't try to fix the blame, fix the problem.

*Responsibilities should not be energized by exhortation or propaganda, but by clearly laid out duties and expectations.

*The key to good staff performance is training; a well-trained staff member will claim the job as his/her own.

*Be a strong advocate for a principled organization with a clear mission and honest people willing to accept accountability in carrying it out.

Saving America

The salvation of the America we know is not with our colleges and universities. It is in the loyalty and good will of ordinary Americans who still believe in America, work hard, love their families, and continue to practice their faith as Christians, Jews, Muslims, even those who do not confess their religious faith— it's getting harder, but these good people have not yet given up:

They need a boost of greater respect for Truth from those who have vowed to lead!

We do not need lessons from an elite band of progressive philosophers or fake news artists or movie stars, dull as ditchwater. We have in our history, groups that exemplify crossing over heroically from tragedy to revival and exoneration and new life purpose and national pride. Some of this history lies with Native American tribes, unfortunately almost completely unknown to the public.

Crazy Horse and Chief Joseph were patriots as honed to the ideas of freedom, liberty and justice as any of the founders of the new nation. Their tragedy stems from the white invaders' belief that they and their way of life had to be crushed in order that the new nation might spread and flourish. Thus ensued America's genocidal movement that none of the Founding Fathers would have approved.

On the walls of the library of Oglala Lakota College in Kyle, South Dakota there is an impressive array of photographs of Oglala young men who served their country in the military forces.

This is a remarkable story. These young Indian Braves began to call America their country, honor the flag, and join the U.S. military less than a generation after Wounded Knee and the end of the massacres. Stories of their courage in combat despite prejudice against them are intriguing and inspiring.

In the last century Native Americans consistently sent more men per capita into the U. S. Armed Forces than any other racial or ethnic group.

One Indian war story that stirred my heart is about Private Clarence Spotted Wood from North Dakota. He was born in 1914, entered the Army in 1942, went overseas in August 1944, and was killed December 21, 1944 in Luxembourg. On January 28, 1945 a memorial service was held in his honor. He had instructed his tribe: " If I should be killed and you have a memorial service, I want soldiers to go ahead with the American flag, I want cowboys to follow, all on horseback, I want one of the cowboys to lead the wildest of our horses with saddle and bridle on, I will be riding that horse." The service was carried out according to his instructions.

My conclusion is that the warrior spirit strong in the blood and culture of the Plains Indians could not die but was transferred to the service of the people who had taken their lands. This may not seem rational or just to those who want logical explanations, but we serve a God of surprises who allows Truth to wind its own path whatever our intentions.

It's a great irony that Native Americans, their lands having been stolen by the white man, became cowboys. The grand myth of the American cowboys and Indians has been played out all over the world. It's the story of the American frontier where the dialectics of America's development were fashioned.

Scots and American Indians

The history of the Scottish Highlanders is marked by their devotion to the land and expression of fighting spirit. I submit that the American Indian (or as some prefer, Native American) was cast from the same mold as the Scottish Highlander.

The tribal social structure with chieftain authority was similar to the Scottish clans. There was savagery but no worse than the European variety. In both tribal and clan culture there was a strong sense of honor, loyalty, family responsibility, and focus on justice.

The Indian had no concept of private property and could not understand how the land could be bought and sold. But again, is this not similar to the Scot cotters' idea that whatever else happened, the land would always be there for them?

As the American West opened up, there was a serious ground of difference between the white man and the red man about land ownership and responsibility that triggered enormous tragedy. In other respects I believe these men could have been brothers and could have found ways to avoid the genocide and the great devastation of nature that marked the 19th century.

Could it all have been done differently in ways that would have synthesized and harmonized the best common values and preserved our natural wealth? Yes, we can see that now in the aftermath, and perhaps there is some salvation through restoration efforts of sterling organizations such as *Earthjustice, Natural Resources Defense Council, National Wildlife Federation, Audubon, Nature Conservancy, and Sierra Club.*

XII

The Braveheart Tradition

In my first trip to Scotland several years ago I visited Inverness and attended a ceilidh there. I was shocked by how emotional it was for the participants. It was as though they were still living the Jacobite rebellion.

For the Scots there were three great battles which established their fighting spirit as indelible. One is Bannockburn (1314), a decisive battle which won their independence ; then they lost it again four centuries later at Culloden(1746), an unmitigated disaster for them against an English army of Scottish mercenaries. In this battle, Scots fought Scots and gained neither victory nor glory, but from this time on, English armies were filled with Scottish soldiers.

The third battle that stamped permanently the fighting spirit of the Scots was the decisive one in the war against Napoleon, the battle of Waterloo(1815). Had England not defeated Napoleon at Waterloo, today we might all be speaking French, just as had we not defeated Hitler we might all be speaking German. But I think that is not the high significance of the battle of Waterloo, for it was not Englishmen who won that battle. It is a great irony, perhaps lost in the history of wars, that the battle of Waterloo was won by young Scottish and Irish soldiers.

On the front lines of battle were Scottish regiments, the Scots Greys, the Cameron Highlanders, the Black Watch, and the Royal Scots Guards. These were concentrations of a fierce race of Highland warriors chosen for the center of battle by the Duke of Wellington for that reason.

. What was that spirit echoed in battle? Was it a battle cry for England? No, these young men of Waterloo (reference those boys of Pointe du Hoc) were not English, they were Scotsmen!

Although they were conscripted into its Army to fight for England, their true allegiance was revealed when they stormed the battlefield and fought and died with this cry out of their throats:

Scotland Forever!

What explains it? This little two-bit nation, perhaps 5 million people, a nation of no great wealth, but a nation with influence far out of proportion to its size, that has bred some of the most outstanding leaders of the western world— Robert Burns of course, voted by Scotland's people in 2000 as the greatest Scotsman who ever lived, and followed by others of equally impressive biographies/or near equal— Adam Smith, Sir Walter Scott, Alexander Graham Bell, Robert Louis Stevenson, John Muir (the great American environmentalist),Robert Adam (the classical architect of supreme elegance), John Paul Jones (father of the American Navy), Tony Blair(recent British Prime Minister) — to mention a few.

Think about this: after Culloden came the Clearances, a time of oppression and famine worse than the Highlanders had ever known, heaped on them by the landed aristocracy. People were evicted from the glens to make way for sheep. Some whole families were thrown out into the snow at the peak of winter. These were the "cotters" that Burns celebrated, now completely betrayed and abandoned because the sheep had the power of money much like oil and gas does today. Does this not seem incredible? Yes, but it is true.

At the beginning, the people accepted their new lot. They held on to the spirit of the clan, hoping to share in the glory of the chief when the Bard sang or the piper played. Their attachment to the land was deep and strong, as deep and permanent as anything could be because they came out of the earth and peopled it with faeries and ugly trolls and mystical warriors of mountain granite. Scottish culture was still virile and immediate. Yet, strangely, they acknowledged the rights of the aristocracy to dispose of them at will. Even the church could not intervene.

The women also shared this love of the land and fighting spirit. From the clan wars, there are brutal and pitiful stories of women forced onto the battlefield. Here is a fifth century Celtic account:

"The work which the best of women had to do was to go to battle and battlefield, and counter and camping, fighting and hosting, wounding and slaying. On one side of her she would carry her bag of provisions, on the other her babe, her wooden pole upon her back, and it had on one end an iron hook, which she would thrust into the tress of some woman in the opposite battalion. Her husband behind her, *carrying a fence stake in his hand and flogging her on to battle. The mother of the Abbot of Holy Iona chanced on a day to come on a battlefield. Such was the thickness of the slaughter into which they came that the soles of the women would touch the neck of another. Though they beheld the battlefield, they saw nothing more touching or pitiful than the head of a woman in one place and the body in another, and her little babe upon the breast of the corpse, a stream of milk upon one of its cheeks and a stream of blood upon the other." (From WJ Watson, "The Celtic Church and Paganism,"* Celtic Review, *1918.)*

This is not an account of heroism, but a reflection of Highland fighting values and myths going far back in centuries. This woman may have died before she was sixteen, but the spirit did not die. The Braveheart tradition —its harsh excesses as well as its glories—was being born in extreme circumstances.

It was inevitable that this structure would collapse, and so the great migration of Scots to all parts of the world began. Many came to America, settled in the mountains not unlike their Highlands, and true to their heritage became the Fighting Scots of our history. They were the best of soldiers because they knew how to take orders, did not flinch in the face of calamity, and always fought with a sense of desperation if not purpose.

XIII

A Valorous Citizenship

I was pondering the following potential disasters as to whether or not we could survive them as United States of America:

nuclear war

massive grid failure

devastating monetary collapse

virtual reality trapping our souls while the natural environment continues to decline

the coming of thinking, self replicating machines

American Civil War II

My personal conclusion is that the country is still strong enough to manage these crises and survive in some form, though perhaps not to our liking, except for the last which would mean the end of our nation.

For a civil war to break out enough people must perceive the situation as unbearable and be willing to use violence. The police must be unwilling or unable to keep the sides apart. Do we have these conditions? Is there evidence of grave danger of their development?

Why do I believe that Americans united could survive any of the potential disasters we are facing in 2018?

Because we are an exceptional nation despite the hard left's ongoing efforts to deny our culture and constitutional government. We are a valorous people who have demonstrated time and again the courage and resiliency to overcome crisis and continue to forge a unique national identity that has made this country the envy of many others.

I make this claim despite the historic egregious errors of our American government.

We see it in the splendid formulation and development of U.S. Constitutional Democracy. Radical Leftists desire to erase this identity and substitute it with they know not what!— merely shows the vapid vision which seeks to bring America to its knees.

We see it in the beginnings of "environmentalism", our national parks, and transportation systems

We can see it in the WWII response of "the Greatest Generation"— the emergence of Rosie the Riviter and the Boys of Pointe Du Hoc—seminal events in our 20th century history.

We can see it in the bravery of police and firefighters who ran toward rather than away from the explosians of 9/11 and in the call of my young friend in Pennsylvania, Todd Beamer, "Let's Roll."

And we see it again in the intrepid spirit of those Southern folks (neighbors all) dealing with the devastation of Hurricanes Harvey and Irma —and further shown in the marvelous support given from citizens all across the nation.

Yes, we have a valorous citizenship! But it is currently deeply divided and not happy with its government.

We have allowed ourselves to be split by poisonous politics and Orwellian doctrine that move us closer to the brother against brother phenomenon of our 1860's Civil War.

WHAT, ME WORRY?

I want to agree with those who say "nothing like that could happen in today's America."

But wait! I worry to think this is just head in the sand philosophy that does not understand how catastrophes are triggered by events that can produce unimagined turmoil. If we have not thought through the possibilities, it is no good later *to "cry havoc."*

It is not my intention here to be a scaremonger, but I refuse to cast aside my duty as a free citizen in a God gifted country to think through our issues and challenges and strive for clarity, even if it seems impossible to arrive there.So I want to take on here, as an example, the realistic threat of massive grid failure caused by " electromagnetic pulses" (EMP)* without any claim to science/ techology expertise. I am just a reporter, hoping to find clarity.

XIV

EMP: A Triggering Catastrophe

A letter from Prof. Richard Andres of National Defense University explains that electromagnetic pulse, EMP, can take two forms: the first comes from extreme solar activity, the second from an enemy detonated nuclear weapon above the atmosphere in the purposive attempt to create an EMP. The origins are different, but either could be catastrophic for the U.S.:

"Research also determined that our systems are unable to respond effectively to an event that knocks out power to a large region or the nation as a whole... Because virtually all financial transactions and communications are now conducted electronically, without electricity regions would lose the ability to buy, sell,and communicate instantly...Most individuals would lose access to food and medicine after around three days. Law enforcement would cease to exist in most localities within a week... Over a year the effects of a nationwide blackout would approach the level of a limited nuclear war."

Prof. Andres concludes that because the Grid is owned and regulated by so many different companies and group, it is the individual states rather than the federal government, that are responsible for protecting against EMP.

It is not easy to assess the probability of EMP occurring in the future, and no one likes to imagine the effects. So it is probably easy, with so many other detectable problems, to ignore this disaster possibility. It is also not hard to recognize that this could be an enormous mistake.

What are the implications for action? First and foremost, as the National Defense University analysis contends, it is up to state and local governments to enact regulations to protect against EMP threats to the Grid. Companies should be required by law to protect themselves. Local communities should have at least some amount of local renewable power generation capabilities that they can fall back on to keep emergency services running during the outage.

Some may say that all of this bureaucratic regulation, which is often unreliable in the first place, will be expensive— probably true. Yet in the face of a real EMP disaster, preparation costs would be negligible in comparison.

If it should occur, I believe the American spirit would kick in again, but I also believe it is simply foolish to depend on this solitary escape.

I believe it is natural for us to pray against it, but if it should occur, the impact would be so harrowing and the tendency to cast blame in all directions so overwhelming, that the unexpected force of it could trigger Civil War.

Such a national catastrophe would be abetted by radical left leaders who would welcome it as the launching of their Socialist agenda for a new America unshackled from the traditional values and institutions they hate and seek to destroy.

XV

Bureaucratic Ineptitude and Lies

"Political language… is designed to make lies sound truthful and murder respectable, and to give an appearance of solidity to pure wind." (George Orwell)

Freedom is under assault in the USA today in unprecedented ways. Corruption in various forms is now rampant, and almost everybody knows it. For those apologists who contend that this has always been true, it may be easy to make this claim in isolated cases but not to same degree, particularly in those institutions relied upon for check and balance, such as our universities, mainstream press, our financial institutions, the Justice Department, State Department, and the White House itself.

Pin blame on bureaucratic incompetence: God knows the IRS, Veterans Affairs, Land Management, EPA, etc. have much to answer for; but ultimately accountability lies with those who wield top level federal authority and power, including the Attorney General, Senate and House Leaders, and the President of the United States.

I have studied and taught and wrote about our history and government and been involved in institutional governance for many years, and have never felt this way before, even during the sad times of the Vietnam War.

Shadow Government

There is a growing concern among many citizens, myself included, about the massive growth of government and its evolution to a shadow government, not elected by the people, what some call "the deep state."— undetectable, hard to describe, but worrisome that it is more than just the problem of bureaucratic incompetence. Our federal government has grown far from what the Founding Fathers intended in the Constitution. In 1954, Sen. William Jenner warned about it:

"Today the path to total dictatorship in the US can be laid by strictly legal means, unseen and unheard by Congress, the President, or the people. Outwardly we have a constitutional government. We have operating within our government and political sphere, a well-organized political action group in this country, determined to destroy our Constitution and establish a one-party state. The important point to remember about this group is not its ideology but its organization. It operates secretly, silently, continuously to transform our government. This group is answerable neither to the president, the Congress, nor the courts. It is practically irremovable."

I am still evaluating the worth of this speech. If it were a definitive appraisal, in my view we would already have reached the border line of the end of days. I do not subscribe to conspiracy theories, but neither do I suggest that we should simply dump Sen. Jenner's argument as irrelevant.

Whatever the facts of it are, it will be a challenge to root it out and restore confidence that we still have government *for the people, by the people, of the people,* and yes, your vote really does count!

The situation is not hopeless!

We should not underestimate the talents and courage and insights of those young people who yearn for a principled government of integrity and honesty. Some may have been led into hypocrisy and deceit, but they are not all "snowflakes." Like most of us, I believe they detest the lies coming out of the mouths of power-hungry politicians. They are caught in a cruel dillemma – – the same old greed, violence and hatred masked by pseudonyms class struggle, racial struggle.

I have worked with the 16-25 age group my whole life and know their essential character: they want friends and are quick to bond w/each other in honesty and fairness; they are united by respect for freedom and equality — intrinsic American values. Sadly, they are being let down by some of their professors who have opted for ideology of class conflict and identity politics— rather than education— threatening to tear us apart as enemies.

Once again, as Orwell warned us, the lie has come upon us.

The liar does not always go straight for the throat ; he/she may ask only for allegiance to the lie, for complicity in the lie, respect for some alleged greater purpose that excuses the lie.

The simple redeeming act of a courageous man or woman is not to take part in the lies. The young man or woman trying to find truth even while recognizing that the search for truth is sometimes a thicket of difficulty, my faith tells me will have God on his/her side.

I think they and all of us need to be reminded of the words of our greatest president, Abraham Lincoln:

"We are not enemies but friends. We must not be enemies. Though passion may have strained it must not break our bonds of affection. The mystic chords of memory stretching from every battlefield and patriot grave to every living human heart and hearthstone all over this broad land, will yet swell the chorus of the union, when again touched, as surely they will be, by the better angels of our nature."

XVI

On Death and Dying
"A lyrical path to the meaning of death"

"Because I could not stop for Death-
He kindly stopped for me-" (Emily Dickinson)

"I long for scenes where man has never trod;
There to abide with my creator, God,
Untroubling and untroubled where I lie;
The grass below— above, the vaulted sky. " (John Clare)

"I have a rendezvous with Death
At some disputed barricade,
When Spring comes back with rustling shade
And apple-blossoms fill the air—
I have a rendezvous with Death
when Spring brings back blue days and fair." (Alan Seegar)

"Death be not proud, though some have called thee
mighty and dreadfull, for thou art not so..." (John Donne)

"I began working as a hospice volunteer after my mother died. I needed to understand death. I came to look death face to face as a hospice volunteer and to transform the pain of death and all the

suffering into a normal step in our life. I learned that in death - for most people - the veil is lifted and we come to know our true self. It is a beautiful thing to see this. I saw it in the eyes and faces of the dying. There is no need to cover up or project the false self - the control, power and ego. You can sense that these signs of the false self don't mean anything anymore and as such there is release and contentment in death. There is peace. " (Tony Lipnicki)

How then shall we live as we approach Death? Is there indeed a noble way?

The simplistic version of dying for a noble cause— dying as the ultimate sacrifice— is portrayed in a song sung for our soldiers in World War II:

"There's a Star-Spangled Banner waving somewhere... only Uncle Sam's brave heroes get to go there... and that's where I want to be when I die." (My Uncle John loved this song.)

Consider an example of a soldier's ultimate sacrifice for God and Country:—

The Boys of Pointe du Hoc— the band of young Rangers who scaled the cliffs in France with German machine gun fire raining down on them— there was no coming back down, they had to go up straight into the hellfire, one of the most significant acts of bravery and sacrifice in our military history.

This heroic view colors our fantasy of death, but it is not normal. Most men do not experience death as a celebration, it is too existential; a far greater number than our war heroes struggle for their dignity. Their lives are unheralded, except perhaps for a family wrouht obituary: most live out their lives in quiet desperation.

But it is a contemptible lie, fomented by ideologues and cowards, to state that men are not motivated to live lives of honor, valor,courage and integrity. Without some hint of this aspiration you cannot be a *real man*.

From My El Salvador Poems /Ranger Jack 1994 :

No torment this, Lord, nor humility,
Still I wonder and ask, could you bear with me
a little in my folly, and indeed bear with me?
Dull sting, earned, leads somewhere,
fixed as a chain to be broken, unwanted desire probes and probes
the Will, face to face with folly, casting aside, spending, urging
the soul to remember, to surrender, bringing what?

Oh, clear pool of water, light refracting leaves, rocks,plants,
Time, what delicate mighty complex
forces have diffused this composition and event?
Unity, form, glorious in God's world,
all with touch of illusion.

Knowledge is power, wealth is power.
There is a power mightier than both of these: Truth.
Thank you, Lord,
for helping me to reflect upon
your truth,
your joy,
your beauty,
your love.

"Why Lord,do men seek danger, when you breathe it into all around us?" These are lines *I* wrote
after an escape in the night and I couldn't understand myself going back to repeat the experience.
Then I came to a piece by Sebastian Junger: "Coulter's Way" explains something that I think only
men can understand— and maybe only a minority of them— it isn't a matter of something good,
bad, right, wrong, it's just something in our nature, a thing some people don't even know exists.
But I have seen it, and I know, God knows.

Christ Memory

In some distant cloud, Lord, is there the memory certain for us to find as ages unfold?
is there a hint of meaning in your time pulling reverie, like seasons, some formula force of meaning's range?
The dual spirit/substance fosters or fails God's truth
akin to the ribbed Mountain that builds and wears?
Goodness, beauty, truth trampled yet increase.
Through a mystic hardness, the Christ memory calls.
Angels know if we do not, though brute force tears
the long night to light of day, it will release.

Yes, there was a time, we feel it's wrench,
when babes bled on mothers' breasts,
short willed, swill bellied priests contempted vows.
Death was kind in the face of Satan's stench,
gold held the highest chair, every heart's chest.
All this come round again?

The Christ memory will not pass away,
what ever lie enslaves,what ever lifeless doctrine
brays in mocking pages,
Joy succeeds, announcing God who saves,
who is, who was,who is to come,
at the end of the ages.

One lost night of charades and schemes of stolen glory,
Death stopped by my door,
not so rich as pain but freer!
And I? Where am I in that parade? You alone, Lord,know the story,
the changing chances at the core,
of all the endings, and the cool prize at my bier.

Just a crack away, some dominion waits for me.
When I go, what sender, lover, destroyer, enemy provides?
Who lifts this arm, God, Is it I or Thee?

Surprised or no, nowhere traces to that divide.
Then lost indeed are we in that lost night,
where the sweetest hopes and dreams
drift like green and gold on ponds,
and all our strivings serve no purpose,
cellular, animal things, nothing beyond,
and we are caught in a faithless pledge.

Yet wait! The red rosebud blossoms,
all in its crimson glory spread,
while a song floats out from somewhere,
someone dear, close to you Lord, emptied purity and light,
bringing life to life, fresh again, though still unclear,
as though rain clouds opening from majestic loving height!

****

I have traveled a lot in my life, seen and done many interesting things. I have a bookmark from Oxford, Arnold's "sweet city with her dreaming spires."

Oxford inspired me. The rugged rocks of Iona, Scotland inspired me. I spent an entire day resting with them. The Genesee Abbey *inspired me.*

The devotion to God exemplified by Trappist monks inspired me.

The monks are like soldiers, standing at the wall for us in their faithfulness to God.

Father Marcellus came to Genesee when he was 22 years old in 1954. For the next 51 years, he has come to prayer and daily worship with his brothers, six times each day, all those days. It is a rigorous life, highly disciplined, but through it the monks find peace and express their love of God. They do not proselytize, but their witness is great. They are real men. Some people may say, to enter this order must be like entering into prison, but that is a mistaken, blindingly superficial view.

God's truth must be discovered. Through a thicket of danger and difficulty It is a lifelong journey of discovery anchored by faith.

The Monks of Tibhirine

The monasteries are beacons of light, not only to the Christian communities, but to the Islamic as well. It is hard to imagine, but the path of universal love and justice for all can lead to peace between these religions where now there is such misunderstanding, distrust, and in some cases, rightly so.

If we need an exact modern date on the launch of the war that brought us world wide terrorism, it began not on 9/11, but on All Saints day, November 1, 1954 in Algeria. 12 killings occurred that day. A year later after the brutal Phillipsville massacre of 250 Europeans, France knew that Algeria was a serious problem. War had been declared.

Whose fault? Who's to blame? At the time, Bishop Duval saw clearly how the seeds of terrorism had been sown. In 1947, he said," you have to be blind not to be terrified at the extent of social injustice and the consequences it must bring." Prophetic words.

It is a huge task to unravel the snarls of injustice, faith, terror, and hatred that grew from that terrible seed.

Flashpoint, now the monster confronting all civilzed people: nothing can pardon, or even explain, the plain evil that anoints islamest savagery and cruelty.There is no compromise; it must be vanquished.The Monks have been there from the beginning,dauntless for the challenge.

God has such men and women.

XVII

"When the music changes the walls of the city shake" (Plato)

I have been a public speaker for a long time, also have written hundreds of essays and letters that express my personal opinions. I agree that anyone who expresses his opinion in public should expect public criticism in return. As the saying goes, " if you can't stand the heat, get out of the kitchen." I am also an advocate of free speech.

If I have any careful readers here, I want to warn you about the following article: never before have I felt any need for it, but I acknowledge that the language I have borrowed here is nasty, vulgar, and needs to be kept away from children. The subject is <u>rap music.</u>

I enjoy all kinds of music: Classical, Baroque, popular, blues, country, bluegrass,gospel, even some rock, but I will not listen to rap music. Rap is an abomination.

I grieve to acknowledge that in saying this I am out of touch with most young people in the world: inexplicably, for many of them this "music" is sacrosanct. If my attitude were known at a rap concert I would probably be in danger.

To place it in analytical context, I will compare it with the message of art presented at an exhibit held a few years ago (following is from a previous article I wrote):

"Sensation" was a much glorified exhibit in London dedicated to "grunge" and "punk" and other crudity that probably was original. One huge painting was of a woman who had tortured and murdered several small children and thus became a celebrity. It hung along with other pornographic paintings of nude women. The mother of one of the slaughtered children protested the exhibit, and indeed there was a lot of outrage about it. (The Brits have not given up yet.) Still it was declared to be a great artistic success because it broke through taboos and set a new standard for art."

That is an example of how depraved our culture has become on the fringes, seemingly irredeemable. Another example is the figure of Jesus on a cross in a bottle of urine.

I submit that rap concerts in their vulgarity— a constant stream of motherfuckers ("mothafuckas"),bitches,whores ("ho's"), dead cops,pigs — are even worse, yet rap lyrics are accepted and praised by connoisseurs who will even have them boldly engraved on buildings, as I have seen in both New York and Rome.

Consider the value of these lines from the song,"Real Niggaz Don't Die"

"I got a case of spittin' in a motherfucker's face...

If every nigga grabbed a nine and started shooting motherfuckers

it would put them in line."

Let me pose a few questions before continuing:

Can I quote from this publicly recorded rap song in a critical vein without being called a racist? Does it open up my writing to censorship? On the other hand, does it push me in the direction of those professors and "snowflakes" calling for censorship on college campuses? Am I in any danger from the new fascists?

To continue: Of course, it is true that a man may be born into difficult circumstances and that often these are unfairly distributed. But it is the duty of every *real man* to make the best of the hand that he is dealt, an obligation that continues through life. No one can get through life without suffering some wrong, some injustice or unfairness— a cause for resentment. But the fact that resentment may in some sense be justified does not make it a proper or constructive engagement with the world.

The most astonishing thing about our culture today is that this rap stuff is not only appreciated, it is praised, and sometimes regarded as heroic. What effect does it have on children? Well, who says that should be a consideration? Does it really fuckin' matter?

Is there another greater righteous cause involved here: is it a booster for the the radical left movement to establish political correctness, end male dominance, purge America of its heroes and icons, get rid of the idea of American exceptionalism, and rewrite American history?

It is a culture gone half-mad. We are fortunate indeed that the other half is still marvelously creative. But it's unclear what is most tendentious? I'm afraid we're sinking further into the muck.

XVIII

The Girls of Tehran

"Thank heaven for little girls
they grow up in the most delightful way."

Delara Derabi was 22 years old in Iranian prison, so now she would have been in her mid 30s, with children of her own, a talented leader in her Muslim community.

I keep pondering why her life was so mercilessly and cruelly and senelessly ended when she had so much to give to her people. Why did the women of her community not come to her aid?

I am intrigued by the basic question of why these girls of Tehran took on the role of moral leadership? When their male brothers and fathers retreated, they held their ground, never free of humiliation or the threat of being flogged and thrown into prison for "their own education and protection." In the streets it is best that they not be seen nor heard, keeping eyes focused on the ground, not daring to look at passersby.

Asar Nafisi, author *of Reading Lolita in Tehran* (2003) explains that the streets are patrolled by militia called the *Blood of God* to make sure that women wear their veils properly, do not wear makeup, and do not walk in public with men who are not their fathers, brothers or husbands. At any moment they may be hurled into a patrol car, taken to jail, flogged, forced to wash toilets and humiliated in other perverse ways. The humiliation of women stems from new sharia law that lowered the age of marriage from 18 to 9, reinstated stoning as punishment for adultery and prostitution, as well as other offenses not clearly defined.

Delara Derabi was sentenced to prison when she was 17, accused of murdering an elderly relative. She was hanged even though she had been given a temporary stay of execution by the Chief Justice. A British journalist reported, "she phoned her mother on the day of her hanging to beg for help and the phone was snatched by a prison official who said, we will easily execute your daughter and there's nothing you can do about it"..." Mother I can see from my window the scaffold where they are going to hang me."

Why do some Muslim women seek to justify honor killings, and forced marriages?

Well, we still have the brave girls of Tehran! Against the massive forces of paranoia, cruelty, and legally validated persecution and violence against women,they are still telling us that this is not a time for hopelessness and despair.

More penetrating, what nameless, inscrutable, unearthly thing is it that causes a man or woman or an entire community to savage and destroy their own children? What explains our own indifference to the suffering of little girls?

Is it really 'nameless'? Can it be explained in simple religious argument as the 'problem of evil"? Is it enough to say that Satan fell out of heaven to ravage God's creation?

I claim no authority on these matters,but I think we must go back millennial times and forces ago in God's creation of the world, from the time he said "Let There Be Light," through all the planetary invention and stardust, space potentiality soaring across an endless pre-biological vista, rainbow clusters of stars turned into nebulas, extraordinary shapes that defy description, indescribable colors, through further reaches of space emanating with the hum of celestial music, and black holes where nothing ever escapes, to the heavens where God releases his dialectical purpose, and a stage is set for His image projection, maybe not the only one, for the kind of life we know.

In blackness evil was born, blackness, all blackness, the primordial existence of natural/material things spurred on to its mysterious development by the immutable principle of "grow or die." God allowed evil to come into the world.

God works through an evolutionary process involving time.Evangelicals seem to insist that the substance of the Trinity could not have evolved; it had to be there from the beginning. Does it not seem to fit the Logos better that God was impersonal and naturally indifferent in the first stage of the universe He was creating?

The natural order came first, and then came what is referred to in the Nicene Creed as the " Holy Spirit, the Lord, the giver of life." This Spirit, as Jesus himself called it, is distinguished from the all powerful Creator and bears no responsibility for the natural order of things. The world was a given.

"In the beginning was the word...
And the word was made flesh...
And dwelt among us...
We have seen his glory
who came from the Father
full of grace and truth." (Gospel of John)

We cannot know how or when exactly: the human creature became self aware— knowing that he knew— thus the emergence of the human soul! For God the Creator it may have been an act similar to the emergence of the first flower: For millions of years vegetation rioted on the earth without flowers; then one morning a flower appeared and soon thereafter this miracle covered the planet in a blaze of glory. It would also be so with humans.

This Deity, sprung from the First, and merciful and caring whereas the First, in a vascular recess of power and majesty was not, became a part of human consciousness imparting an awareness of the Divine Presence and making us forever capable of faith and hope and love.

In framing this miracle, I realize that I am a heretic in the eyes of many followers of Christ Jesus. But I believe I am faithful to truth, as God leads me, in this attempt to reconcile rational understanding and acceptance of the divine mystery...even in the context of trying to find an answer to the evil done to the girls of Tehran and countless others.

I accept the possibility of my error but to finish, I cannot accept any idea of forgiveness or an apologetic for those bastards who raped and brutalized little girls: They need to rot in hell!

XIX

Lessons from A Super Bird

**"When one tugs at a single thing in nature, he finds it
attached to the rest of the world." (John Muir)**

My books on *Chasing Crazy Horse* are full of episodes of betrayal of Native Americans and the land they revered. There are many environmental lessons that have relevance to the questions involved in End of Days. But the lesson I like best illustrates the love of God and the intricate energies He gave that some call "systems" (and indeed they are), in a life story of a little bird.

My backyard has become a great hatching area for sparrows. Each summer evening I watch flights of hundreds of them, flying across the yard to their roosting places in the Box Elders and Cedars. I call to them and wonder why they don't pay attention to me since I am the provider of approximately 25 pounds of seed for them every week. But they have resigned me to the role of observer and nothing more. Still, once in a while I spot a particular bird in the bush at my window who has fattened on my feed and preens a sleek brown feather coat. He is an athlete, only a couple of ounces in weight but a survivor in his bird world.

I am attracted to him because he reminds me of a world champion bird of incredible strength and brilliance who travels in a much more expansive realm, immeasurable by our means, up-and-down the entire planet Earth. By his conquering of it he is not only a victor but a messenger of the mystery and power of nature.

He is a mighty robin -sized shorebird, weighing in at 4 1/2 ounces, a Rufa red knot by classification. I discovered his story in a book by Philip Hoose, *Moon Bird: a Year on the Wind with the Great Survivor B- 95.*

Each February B-95 takes off with his flock of 1000+ Rufa red knot companions from their winter ground in the Tierra del Fuego (southern tip of South America) for a journey of 9000 miles to their breeding ground in the Canadian Arctic. Late in summer they begin the return journey, 9000 miles back to where they started.

Why do they do that? Why don't they stay in one place and live and adapt as other creatures do? How are they able to navigate unerringly such a journey? And a special question: B- 95 has made the journey nearly 20 times; how much longer can he do it? What gives him such amazing power and longevity?

There is more than one story involved with Moon Bird. There is the individual survival story of B-95. There is the story of the great bird migrations. There is the story of dedicated scientists such as Patricia Gonzalez and Brian Harrington and their colleagues who bring the glory of the red knots into our lives. And there is a looming story of extinction.

In the 20 years B-95 has been flying, the Rufa red knot population has declined by 80%. Bird scientists declare that the main reason for the sharp decline is that the stopover sites for migratory shorebirds are being littered with trash, dug up, polluted, poisoned and otherwise degraded. It is a serious question if we shall see shorebirds in the future.

Happening now is a mass distinction of many species. It is not the first time in the history of the world that this has occurred. But the extinction wave happening now is different: It may be likened to the extermination of the American bison in the 19th century. At the beginning of that century there were over 50 million Buffalo roaming the planes. By the end of the century there were a few hundred left struggling for survival in the Yellowstone.

One species— Homo sapiens— is responsible for wiping out thousands of life forms by consuming more than half of the world's freshwater, radically altering the Earth's resources, and indiscriminate slaughter. Commandeers for new wells are no longer satisfied with the traditional methods of land and water exploitation. Now there are new techniques of hydraulic fracturing deep into the earth and the oceans without real knowledge or regard for long-term consequences. In this context, extinction of the shorebirds may be a minor consequence, hardly worth noticing.

Why should we care about shorebirds? Why care about anything that does not benefit us directly or give us pleasure? Before we were knowledgeable enough even to raise such questions, the American Indians knew the answer. Everything is connected! And behind the material things of this earth there is a Great Spirit that does not bless destruction or clumsy rearrangements of His creation.

Each species belongs to a complicated web of energy and activity called an eco- system. Together, these webs connect everything from the smallest, most obscure living things to the big trees and rivers and mountains, the kings of our environment. We do not know how these eco- systems can be unraveled or the consequences of that happening. Yet God gives us examples of the mystery and the power. One such example is the fascinating little Super Bird, B- 95.

Every life form is fascinating and mysterious in its own right, and each species with which we share the Earth is a success story. The Lord God made them all and made them to work according to His design. It's the responsibility of Homo sapiens to understand and protect them. And, yes, to enjoy them! just as I enjoy the sparrows in my backyard.

And just to replicate on the power of love, here is another story about another little bird, taken from "Sketches from the Underground", by Ivan Turgenov:

Only By Love

I was on my way home from hunting, and was walking up the garden Avenue. My dog was running in front of me. Suddenly he slackened his pace and began to steal forward as though he scented game ahead.

I looked along the Avenue, and I saw on the ground a young sparrow. It had fallen from the nest (a strong wind was blowing and shaking the birches of the avenue), and there it sat and never stirred, except to sketch out its little have grown wings in a helpless flutter.

My dog was slowly approaching it, when suddenly, darting from the tree overhead, an old black throated sparrow dropped like a stone right before his nose, and, all rumpled and flustered, with a plaintive desperate cry flung itself, once, twice, at his open jaws with their great teeth.

It would save its young one; it screened it with its own body; the tiny frame quivered with terror; the little cries grew wild and hoarse; it sank and died. It had sacrificed itself.

What a huge monster the dog must have seemed to it! And yet it could not stay up there on it's safe bough. A power stronger than its own will tore it away.

My dog stood still, and then slunk back disconcerted. Plainly, he too had to recognize that power. I called him to me, and a feeling of reverence came over me as I passed on.

Yes, do not laugh. It was really reverence I felt before that heroic little bird and the passionate outburst of its love.

Love, I thought, is verily stronger than death and the terror of death. By love, only by love, is life sustained and moved. (Ivan Turgenev)

****

There is a question about reality constantly before us, so pervasive and so simple, it's on the lips of every child: "Do you love me?" Where does this come from?

XX

Cowardice and Courage

Are terrorists cowards? I don't usually agree with the comedian, Bill Maher, but I do grant that a comment he made on this topic is astute*:" We have been the cowards, lobbing cruise missiles from 2000 miles away. That's cowardly. Staying in the airplane when it hits the building, say what you want about it, that's not cowardly. Stupid maybe but not cowardly."*

If he had said, *"Evil! but not cowardly, I could partially agree with him."* The problem is, we could easily then get turned to the argument that the terrorists exhibit courage. That's bullshit!

I first wrote on this topic in 2004 in an article titled," *Misbegotten Respect for Suicide Bombers.*" I reported on a worldwide conference of Islamic leaders whose major conclusion was that terrorism should be defined by the United Nations but then went on to proclaim that they were opposed to all forms of terrorism <u>except the Palestinian suicide bombers: they were not terrorists, they were religious martyrs.</u>

Here we have it all again: the deconstruction of logical thought combined with lack of any standard of humanity. How any religious leader can argue that intentional and indiscriminate killing not of soldiers but of innocent people, including children, is justifiable by a higher cause is indeed difficult to understand.

If the ongoing effort to define terrorism should exclude these heinous acts, it is hard to see anything but an apocalyptic end. Such a reigning religious doctrine— already being taught to eight-year-olds in Palestine— would bring the most brutish human condition the world has yet known. For if such a monstrous evil did dominate the human heart, how could there be any room for forgiveness and atonement?

Courage in the right classical sense is a virtue. What the terrorists do is not virtuous by any definition other than the hard left wing disposition to sophistry.

Until our moral discourse became so impoverished that we find it difficult to distinguish between good and evil, we could recognize the difference between the killing of innocents and defending them. Regardless of their claim of pursuing a noble religious cause, the terrorists are engaged in a great evil which is never justified nor neutralized by religious dogma!

I think that a terrorist may indeed be a tough bastard, and any soldier going up against him ought to take that into consideration, but he is never courageous and it is a perversion of our language, not to mention a slander of our first responders and the military to dignify his sin with that label.

There seems to be a tendency, at least in the European states who seek to justify their appeasement— and maybe cowardice— by allowing terrorists, and here in the U.S. traitors like Bowe Bergdahl, some lenience in their actions, which we all should know by now end up by slitting innocent people's throats and torturing children to death.

Why put up with this cognitive dissonance? Is it another aspect of our current ideological stupidity wrought by moral relativism and political correctness?

Let's not get caught in the soporific argument that a person may have desirable and undesirable traits at the same time. Maybe all honest people could admit to that, but I believe the honest man or woman would not confuse courage with an evil act if he/she knows the bloody facts.

XXI
On Death and Dying II

In an article I published in 2009, I wrote the following:

"It seems to me a remarkable coincidence that the Pope and Terri Schiavo died in the same week. In the Pope's mind, Terri was a victim of the culture of death. Although he could see the complexity of issues surrounding the technology of keeping people on permanent life support, he held that there is absolute moral law against both suicide and the killing of a patient by the deprivation of basic human needs of food, water, air, and warmth. If in a mercy killing there is a right to deprive someone of food and water, why not get it over with by putting a bag over the head to deprive the person of air?"

There are many topics on which decent people may disagree and some topics on which a person may not entirely agree even with him/herself, insofar as he/she can see both sides of the argument at the same time. One such topic is that of assisted suicide and euthanasia. I can conceive of circumstances in which I would want it for myself, and circumstances in which it would be the kindest thing for others, and yet, at the same time I understand the objections to it, superbly conveyed in the message from John Paul II above.

I think my conviction is not compromised by suggesting that our alliance with science in nearly all fields may fail to recognize that prescientific knowledge may grasp as well the basic problems of humankind, including death and dying, and the elemental problem of evil.

"Ah, sweet mystery of life at last I found you." Really? Let's take stock for a minute: primitive man's intelligence was no less than our own. Religion once explained the world totally: the reality of that view was no more or less imitative or qualified than the scientific view of reality. With all of the science, why is humankind not experiencing a polar humanity? Do we begin to see the betrayal and false profoundness in behaviorist psychology with all of its manipulative suggestions? Can we begin to see that the driving force behind the mystery of life includes more than reason alone? and more than dogma alone?

The entirety of human history shows that humankind has always been engulfed by the enormity of the problem of evil. However intensive or spiritually guided the effort may be to explain the human condition, we are never lifted out of alienation. Is this true?

First Jesus Christ, then other men of God have recognized the separateness and miraculousness of a spiritual reality which we, by tapping into it, may genuinely be lifted out of alienation and transformed. There is a heroic, individualistic propensity of men and women to risk greatly, sometimes even death, for what is not survival nor escape from evil but spiritual achievement through that primal and universal "psychic energy" that floods the universe.

Is the power of love greater than the power of death? The pessimist, probably in line with the majority, is far less fascinated by love than by death.

The mystery of God and human destiny are beyond science and religion in their separate spheres, but we remain forever heroic creatures who cannot relinquish hope and keep on following a crooked spiritual path, sometimes just an animalistic one.

Yet, somehow by faith and love we are able to reduce skepticism and cynicism, the great eroders of the human spirit. The human condition may be such that man/woman cannot escape suffering and alienation, even with super intelligence, except as he /she finally finds the mercy and grace of God. It may be that for all our efforts, the books cannot be balanced except in afterlife, if there is such a place. Human efforts, however, need not be trivial. Even in microcosm, all of Western philosophy has dealt with the problem of evil and the values of community and loyalty and integrity and dignity and love.

"Someday, after we have mastered the winds, the waves, the tides, and gravity we shall harness for God the energies of love: and then for the second time in the history of the world... Man will have discovered fire." (Teilhard de Chardin)

XXII

Mystical Truth

There is a story from the island of Harris in the Outer Hebrides, Scotland, told by the Celtic writer, David Adam, about a leper woman who was an outcast from society, vanished from her Highland home to live on the seashore. Left alone on the island, she discovered that she was not alone. Nothing could separate her from the immanent God,through whom she lived and moved and had her being. The Christ had come to Harris in the woman's aloneness. In some mystical way, she discovered God incarnate in His creation and was uplifted.

> The light shone in her dark days. In her own self she discovered the meaning of the biblical expression, "the word made flesh and dwelling among us."

> In our earthbound/deskbound prison, it is easy to reject or dismiss the Harris woman's story as irreconcilable with rational understanding. Mysticism, while curious at best, is of no real account. To dwell on mystical things is a sure way to be judged odd. Yet these stories will not dry up.

Creation's Big Bang

Myth is a reflection on reality, a way of explaining through generations what actually happened. Let's take an example: At the center of every civilization is a remarkably similar Creation myth. Basically, it is an account of how the world came to be as a gift from God. In primitive times, when it was feared that the gift would be taken back, human sacrifice was offered. To ensure that spring would come again, a king or deity would be taken into the hills to be torn apart and scattered. The world was saved in a Dionysian frenzy.

On April 23, 1992, George F Smoot of Lawrence Berkeley laboratory announced that NASA's Cosmic Background Explorer (COBE) had detected ripples of the Big Bang, the birth of the universe. Scientific debate about creation will no doubt continue. After all the story of creation is very old, and there is no reason to assume that humans will find uncontestable answers that will settle eternal questions.

But the COBE discovery is one that we ought not to pass over lightly. We need to be alert to new knowledge and humbled by it at the same time. Big Bang theory holds that the universe came into being as a result of a primordial explosion and expansion in a tiny fraction of a second(1032), there are several models, but the one which seems most reinforced by the COBE data shows that the first galaxies appeared about 1 billion years later. The universe is now about 15 billion years old.

Except for the cosmologist, using these figures is mind-boggling. That is one reason perhaps to be humble: we can't really grasp the concept of time. A second thing to consider is that the science which brings us such startling information does not call for belief.. Science is constantly replacing theories and opening up new mysteries. It is nevertheless interesting to see how closely the Big Bang Theory, as it is tested, resembles the scriptural account of creation in the Book of Genesis.

George Smoot commented, what we have found is evidence for the birth of the universe. If you're religious it is like looking at God. I'm not sure he meant that, but what he describes easily confirms the faith that there is a God outside of nature, Who fired the world into motion, to create being out of nothing, and transcends it still.

****

I remember years ago when I was a young history professor being profoundly impressed by the story of Victor Frankl's survival in a German concentration camp during World War II. The suffering he endured would have been unbearable except for his remembrance of his beloved wife, whom he could not know was alive or dead. One day, while working in unbearable cold, his soul dying, Frankl received confirmation that communion with his wife was real. In that moment he was restored to life for he knew that his wife was still alive and returned his love:

"The guard passed by, insulting me, and once again I communed with my beloved. More and more I felt that she was present, that she was really with me; I had the feeling that I was able to touch her, able to stretch out my hand and grasped her. The feeling was very strong: she was there. Then at that very moment, a bird flew down silently and perched just in front of me, on the lump of sod which I had dug up from the ditch, and looked steadily at me."

For Frankl it was a moment of reality, fragile as life itself but hard as stone. Here is God's miraculous love with the power of resurrection no science can match, at least so it seemed to me in that first reading, and remains so.

If the world around you seems to be steering wildly off the rails, think on these mystical things of God's love, and recall Shakespeare's line, "there are more things in heaven and earth than are dreamt of in your philosophy."

XXIII

Burns and Yeats

Selecting my favorite poets is difficult to do, and on another day, it may be others but always be in contention would be Robert Burns and William Butler Yeats.They draw me because of their life stories as well as the distinction of their works.

Burns

The memory of Robert Burns has been fondly proclaimed at suppers on his birthday for the past 250 years. He is the only poet honored in this way; even Shakespeare does not get this annual attention.

In Burns' short turbulent life, he produced poems now universally admired, published a book of poetry in the Scots dialect, thus preserving an ancient tongue, revised and wrote over 300 Scots songs, including what has become the world's anthem, *Auld Lang Syne,* wrote over 700 letters in superb standard English, including some of the most beautiful love letters ever written.

His lyrical legacy is all the more remarkable because many of his writings were inspired when he was working the land, filling a life of hardship which he described most aptly as," the cheerless gloom of a hermit with the unceasing toil of a galley slave."

What explains Robert Burns? By the time he was 16 he had read his way through much of classical literature— Shakespeare, Alexander Pope, John Locke and Scottish poets who had preceded him— and he learned Latin, all with not much more than a year of formal schooling. Yes, he was naturally bright, and he was a dedicated scholar, but that does not quite explain him.

The first key to understanding his growth and development is that he had been taught to read! Indeed, it was demanded of him by the church established during the Scottish Reformation led by the religious radical, John Knox, a preacher of truly terrifying power, who insisted that all boys and girls must be taught to read Holy Scripture. As a result, Scotland's literacy rate the end of the 18th century would be the highest in all of Europe— astonishing, because in Burns' time, Scotland was one of the poorest of countries, with a population of about 2 million people. Yet the value placed on reading and writing for religious reasons turned it into a remarkably literate culture.

What old John Knox did not foresee is that once an individual is taught to read, his mind is free, and he begins to make his own decisions about what to read and write and think. The expression, *free to think for oursel's,* has origins in Scotland.

And Burns pushed it to the limit, sometimes beyond, which could land him in trouble with the Kirk or the Court. Burns was always a beacon of controversy. As the saying goes, "he was far ahead of his time." Among his immortal poems, *A Man's a Man,* is one of the most powerful statements ever written on the fundamental dignity and integrity of all men everywhere.

Nor did Burns neglect the majesty of women. Long before our shallow era of political correctness, at a time when Thomas Paine's revolutionary pamphlet, "The Rights of Man", was flooding Europe, Burns wrote his poem, "The Rights of Women."

Burns had a rare insight into the hearts and minds of his fellow Scots that he learned to apply to all people everywhere, regardless of class distinctions or stations in society.

Robert Burns died too soon, at the age of 37. He told his wife, Jean, at the end,"Don't be afraid: I'll be more respected in 100 years after I am dead than I am now." He was not and does not need to be made into a poet superhero, but through his poems and songs, he brought wisdom and grace that made him a legend in his time and likely will continue on for generations to come.

Yeats

William Butler Yeats was born in Dublin, Ireland into a sophisticated but not wealthy Anglo- Irish family well known in art and religious circles. His father was a complete skeptic, rejecting religious belief entirely, fiercely intellectual, and a prominent artist. Yeats, the poet, was influenced both positively and negatively by his father. Out of his own need for belief in revelation and a higher power, he rejected his father's intellectual skepticism, but he did not turn back to the church.

I think of him as the Mozart of poetry. His metaphorical imagery is clear, crystalline, sometimes hard, sometimes soft, often brilliant. There are two convoluted terms that we need to understand Yeats— "dialectical thinking and antinomies." The dialectic is the notion that for every force(thesis) there is a counterforce(anti-thesis). Antinomies are contradictions between principles that seem equally necessary and reasonable.(To a hardened rationalist, it may be unseemly that truth should act in this way, but she does.)

These combine as the best description of Yeats' approach in all his roles, as a poet, dramatist, theater founder and director, Irish Senator and political leader, Nobel Laureate, and lecturer of world renown. His thought was profoundly dialectical. For every truth, he looked for a counter truth, a truth that contradicted the first truth.

Yeats'stance was always heroic, Promethean, even facing certain defeat. His tenacity sprang from a strong belief in the value of Celtic tradition and his commitment to heroic art. He worked through his philosophy and belief to creative, mystical vision. He tried to create his own religion, resorting to various occult forms, including his wife's automatic writing.

In the end, Yeats failed in his quest for a spiritual framework. He failed in my view for the reasons that Alexander Solzhenitsyn articulated many years later in his Nobel address: an artist who attempts to create an independent spiritual world simply *"breaks down, because no man, even a genius, is capable of bearing such a burden— the whole irrationality of art, it's blinding convolutions, it's unpredictable discoveries, it's shattering impact on people, are too magical to be exhausted by the philosophy of any one artist."(Solzhenitsyn)*

Yet where Yeats may have failed philosophically in his system, he created a body of poems of the greatest power and beauty. They are nothing less than miraculous in their aesthetic revelation. In my opinion, "The wild Swans at Coole" is the most beautiful lyrical poem ever written.

Yeats was romantically and politically involved with Maud Gonne for most of his life. She was 6 feet tall and beautiful, some said the greatest beauty in Ireland, of regal bearing, politically very intense. She was a passionate and fearless speaker and campaigner. Yeats thought that she could be Ireland's Joan of arc. In the Victorian age, long before women's liberation, she was indeed a liberated woman.

Politically, Yeats was a "right-winger." He was too much of the poet rejecting violence to be a revolutionary fighter,still he could not escape becoming involved in the politics of Ireland and England.He was on top of the issues, but also conflicted by the violence. He saw that the blood of the Easter 1916 rebellion radically changed everything:

> **"All's changed, changed utterly,**
> **a terrible beauty is born."**

In 1919, when Ireland was in Civil War and World War I was raging in Europe, Yeats' vision turned apocalyptic. The result was a poem of great power, *The Second Coming*, with lines marmolean and unforgettable that seem to fit every generation.

> *... The blood -dimmed tide is loosed, and everywhere*
> the ceremony of innocence is drowned.
> *The best lack all conviction, while the worst*
> *are full of passionate intensity...*

He died in 1939 at age 73, having written his own epitaph:

> *Cast a cold eye*
> *on life, on death.*
> *Horseman, pass by.*

XXIV
The Message of John Paul II

I attended the funeral of Pope John Paul II in Rome and experienced first hand the deep love of this man by thousands present from all over the world. History will remember him as spiritual guardian of the sanctity of life and great moral leader and teacher of the salvific power of faith. I was especially impressed by the large number of young people who attended.: A 20-year-old boy flew to the Vatican and slept in the street. Asked why he was there, he replied, "to pay my respects to the Pope. If I don't see him today I'll be back tomorrow." A beautiful young girl from Kraków, Poland said," I don't know how we can go on without him. He was my Father."

Hope is always present as a measure of faith in a loving God. We cannot know for certain how God may intervene and through what instruments, revealed as opportunities. Even when things are most bewildering, there are spiritual, moral, and intellectual forces which can be marshaled.

The evidence of things hoped for and made manifest is revealed in the faith and work of John Paul II. He understood that, despite Europe's Christophobia, it was Christianity that brought the values of human dignity and laid the foundation for the ideas of democracy and liberty.

In *Ecclesia Europa*, John Paul called his fellow Europeans to courage and hope:

"Do not be afraid! The gospel is not against you but for you... Throughout the vicissitudes of your history, yesterday and today, it is the light which illuminates and directs your way. It is the strength which sustains you in trials. It is the prophecy of a new world, the sign of

a new beginning. It is the invitation to everyone, believers and unbelievers alike, to blaze trails leading to a Europe of the spirit in order to make the continent a true, common home filled with the joy of life."(Quoted in George Weigel, The Cube and the Cathedral, 2005)

This message is universal. Those who are ready to give up on the complexity of our situation, those who cannot see beyond the next day or even the next hour, can find renewal in serious reflection of it.

It was John Paul, more than any other leader, including Ronald Reagan, who was responsible for the collapse of communism in Eastern Europe and ultimately the demise of the Soviet Union. When Europe had forgotten God and started on its path of hopelessness, the communist empire was in its ascendancy. The new religion of communism counted all power in material terms. When Stalin was asked if he should be concerned about what the Pope had to say, his response was classic: " How many divisions does Pope have?"

In the 1990's, John Paul was joined by Billy Graham. Though different in style, both were powerful, influential voices in spreading a message of hope, much needed in Europe.

Europe is now struggling and may not survive in the wake of 20th century reliance on relativism, secularism and materialism. The enemy at the gate is homegrown, inbred Islamist terrorists, justified by ardent corruption of true Islam. This barbarism can be defeated, but Europe does not know how ; it's possible that America does not know how either, having already breathed in Europe's problem. But I believe that America can remain the best hope of the world.

Visits to London and Scotland used to be a restorative pleasure for me. I enjoyed chatting with the "natives" there and could feel the pride in their culture, but no longer. I worry mainly that Britain does not have a residual spirit of traditional values that I can still see in American youth, if it faces up to its own ideolgical threats.

It has always been when things look their darkest that new leadership emerges, as for example, when Patrick again finally reached the shores of Ireland, destined to become the savior of classical antiquity in a dark age. Behind him was the break of day!

John Paul reminds us that Christ is calling us now as He did Patrick, and that God's gifts of beauty and unfailing love and healing power are with us!

My heart goes out to those young people yearning for freedom in places like Iran, Syria, and Russia. Let's not discount the possibility of spiritual intervention.

We face a dark complexity in a split world. Yet, despite our bewilderment, I believe the balance will swing again. Our part, friends, is to summon the courage to continue facing up to the challenge, that, after all, is not an excuse for slinking off and doing nothing.

XXV
Russian Poetry (English translations)

"In the struggle against lies, art has always won and always will. Lies can stand up against much in the world but not against art."

(Alexander Solzhenitsyn)

If I were to do over my early education, I would learn Latin and Russian. They are both essential to a literary career.

Does someone who does not speak Russian have any authority to comment on Russian poetry? Given the difficulty of translations— Vladimar Nabokov called it, "the pathetic business of translating"— the tide runs against it. On the other hand we can hardly do without translators, or at least I cannot, and so with some hesitation and apology and with much appreciation to the great Russian writer, Alexander Solzhenitsyn, I offer these introductions to some poems which seem to me to have too much striking power even in English to be ignored. The poets are Osip Mandelstam,Mikhail Lermontov, and Yevgeny Yevtushenko.

Though disparaged in the West, Solzhenitsyn did more than any other writer to reveal the horrors of the Stalinist regime. From the "Gulag" where he was a "zek" (prison inmate), he brought word of tortures, such as..." prisoners skulls squeezed within iron rings, being lowered into an acid bath, a red hot ramrod trust up their anal canal, a man's genitals slowly crushed beneath the toe of a jackboot..." If these descriptions seem too terrible to read about, perhaps we have a small glimpse of the "zek" experience.

Solzhenitsyn remarks," These people who had experienced on their own hides 24 years of "communist happiness",knew by 1941 what as yet no one else in the world knew: that nowhere on the planet, nowhere in history, was there a regime more vicious, more bloodthirsty, and at the same time more cunning and ingenious than the Bolshevik, the self-styled Soviet regime." (Quoted by Algis Valiunos in *Starlight in Hell, First Things, May 2009.)*

But Solzhenitsyn of course is far from being just a reporter; he is another of the great contributors to the art and the soul of Russian literature, which teaches us so much about our humanity and inhumanity. So too these poets for whom he provides clear context.

The following poem by Osip Mandelstam was circulated by his friends through memory because the words could not be written down. Eventually, they were traced and Mandelstam suffered the fate of millions of others in the "Kremlin mountaineer's"(Stalin's)Russia.

(Quoted in Robert Littell, *The Stalin Epigram, 2009):*

"We live, deaf to the land beneath us,
ten steps away no one hears our speeches.
All we hear is the Kremlin mountaineer,
the murderer and peasant- slayer. ..
Around him a rabble of thin-necked leaders,
fawning half -men for him to play with...
One by one forging his laws, to be flung
like horseshoes at the head, the eye or the groin."

Lermantov (1814-1841) was a romantic poet who rendered a prophetic image of Russia in this poem, *Prediction, quite* remarkable in view of its fulfillment a century later.

"The day will come, for Russia that dark day

when the Czar's diadem will fall, and they,
rabble who loved him once, will love no more.
And many will subsist on death and gore...
Dawn on the streams will shed a crimson light.
And then will be revealed the Man of might
whom thou wilt know, and thou wilt understand
wherefore a shining blade is in his hand..."

Abbreviated Translation by RM French

(what a hell of a poem!)

Lermontov's poem is in Nicholas Berdyaev, *The Origin of Russian Communism, 1948*. Berdyaev, a Russian philosopher and historian,also provides insight to the fanatical Bolshevik mind in his characterization of the revolutionary Nechaev:

"The revolutionary is the doomed man. He has no personal interests, business, feelings, connections, property, or even name. Everything in him is in the grip of one exclusive interest, one thought, one passion, <u>revolution.</u> The revolutionary has broken with the civil order, with the civilized world, and with the morals of the world. He lives in this world in order to destroy it. He must not even love the sciences of this world; he knows one science only, the science of destruction. To the revolutionary everything is moral which serves the revolution— words which Lenin repeated later."

Of a different style, perhaps because a later generation, is Yevgeny Yevtushenko, born in Siberia in 1933. He escaped persecution in his own country and came to America where he was a popular writer and lecturer at American universities. He nevertheless reveals that he has the Russian memory in his poem, *Babii Yar*. Babii Yar is a ravine in Kiev, capital of Ukraine, where over 33,000 Jews were taken and massacred during World War II by German Gestapo.

"The wild grasses rustle over Babii Yar.
The trees look ominous,like judges.
Here all things scream silently,and I myself
am one massive, soundless scream

above the thousand thousand buried here.
I am each old man,here shot dead.
I am every child, here shot dead.
Nothing in me shall ever forget!

Abbreviated Translation by George Reavey

Another poem by Yevtushenko worth reading by any student or teacher:

Lies

"Lying to the young is wrong.
Proving to them that lies are true is wrong.
Telling them that God's in his heaven
and all's well with the world is wrong...
Tell them the difficulties can't be counted,
and let them see not only what will be
but see with clarity these present times...
Say obstacles exist they must encounter,
sorrow comes, hardship happens."

Abbreviated Translation by Robin Milner-Gulland and Peter Levi

XXVI
Russian Poetry II: Solzhenitsyn

"One word of truth outweighs the whole world."

Among the most remarkable life stories, there is Alexander Solzhenitsyn. You should know about this man. Solzhenitsyn is a Russian writer, sentenced to a Russian concentration camp, exiled from the former Soviet Union in 1974. In 1970 he was given the Nobel Prize for Literature.

His Nobel Prize Address, *One Word of Truth,* is a stunning portrayal of the power of art and literature to defeat the lie, clearly one of the most profound and stirring documents on universal freedom ever written. Solzhenitsyn is both a great writer and a prophet. What makes Solzhenitsyn so remarkable is that not only is he a writer with a total worldview, he has made a direct connection between literature and morality, not as a propagandist, as so many writers do, but as a true artist. His works express universal values and will live on.

What is it that a writer should write about? Not political issues of the day, for these are likely to be short-lived. Rather the writer as artist goes to universal themes, essential questions about humanity, inevitably conflict of good and evil.

Solzhenitsyn shows that the evil man is not set apart. He begins, believing that he is doing good, or at least is acting in accord with approved ways. Solzhenitsyn explains the relationship between good and evil and the crossing over, going to an irretrievable condition of evil. With powerful insight, he revealed the root of evil in the 20th century as unconstrained ideology. Unfortunately, it continues in the 21st century. What can we learn from Solzhenitsyn's strong voice and example?

Solzhenitsyn saw freedom as spiritual, not political in nature. His theory of art rests on two fundamental concepts: 1) truth is absolute 2)reality is objective. Both ideas grow from belief in a personal God who created and sustains the world. Art is a gift from God.

In contrast with this view, other artists have seen themselves as creators of independent spiritual worlds. They are doomed to failure by Solzhenitsyn's view, because lacking orientation to a personal God, they have no moral order to rely upon and so drift into confusion and despair.

In the Gulag Archipelago, Solzhenitsyn wrote about an entire country that was brutalized and annihilated by a cruel and inhumane system. Enduring humanity is one of Solzhenitsyn's themes. Human freedom and goodness can live in the human soul, despite degradation and suffering, and can triumph. His own life proves it, as do the lives of Nelson Mandela and Vaclav Havel.

So when Solzhenitsyn was exiled and came to the west, he was astonished to see a different kind of enslavement. He was not grateful for his new freedom. He saw that Western materialistic values have led to greed, corruption, and alienation from God, all destroying the human spirit as much as concentration camps do.

Solzhenitsyn probed the truth of the human condition and experience in the 20th century with great power and moral vision. No writer is more worthy of your attention.

This remarkable poem by Solzhenitsyn, having endured the Soviet Gulag concentration camps, is testimony to the connections of faith and courage and grace:

"How easy it is to live with You, oh Lord,
how easy it is to believe in You.
When my spirit is overwhelmed within me,
when even the clearest see no further than the night,
and know not what to do tomorrow,

You bestow on me this certitude
that You exist and are mindful of me,
that all the paths of righteousness are not barred..."

Solzhenitsyn died in Moscow on August 8, 2003 at age 89. In his last years, somehow he reconciled with the government of Russia. Although some of his final statements are perplexing, it is not too difficult to understand the historical context in which he laid his argument.

The Harvard historian, Crane Brinton, framed a theory of the stages of revolution that shows the last stage as a dialectical return to the state that had existed historically. To recognize history's hold does not refute or contradict the idea of spiritual freedom existing bilaterally with authoritarian tradition. Of course it remains to be seen what politics and action shall develop in Russia, but it is encouraging to note that one year after the death of Solzhenitsyn, *Gulag Archipelago* was adopted into the Russian school curriculum as required reading for all students.

XXVII
Cosmic Consciousness

How do the mystical examples I have used relate to the greater reality of the universe? <u>Here I must explain what I believe.</u>

I believe in evolution as I believe in God. Both physically and spiritually, God uses an evolutionary process in His creation. The primordial nature of God (or the Divine Eros) is the urge to change— "the force that through the green fuse drives"as Dylan Thomas put it— to realize new possibilities, spiritual, not just physical— the immutable principle of *grow or die*.

Tempus Dei Gratia

He is a God of surprises and paradox. Yet, as Herman Melville said, we may surprise him as much as he surprises us. I also accept the poetic argument of WB Yeats that the process is dialectical. In other words, God has two poles or opposites which may be in conflict but strive for synthesis.He has allowed evil to come into the world, but Jesus died on the cross for love. Like many others with so little knowledge, I just accept the mystery of it. God is love; there is no other explanation. Love evolved with the human soul when God decided to become "three persons in one." The acceptance of the Trinity is the core of my belief.

If my belief is true, it can be reconciled with any truth given by science. At the same time I am not willing to stay in a worldview that seeks to bend everything to natural interpretation and cannot see the paradox and mystery in the way God works His will.

I confess to a degree of mysticism, yet it is reconcilable in my mind with rational understanding. I do not mean that the mystical examples I cite are the foundation of my belief in the Trinity. In His primordial nature, God was the First Cause, the Primary Mover. Through the "Big Bang," God fired the universe into motion billions of years ago.

A few years ago, Steven Hawking, probobly the greatest scientist of the 20ih Century, spoke of his work as finding "the mind of God." More recently, he apparently concluded that there is no place for God in the creation of the physical universe. I shudder before the knowledge and courage of a Hawking, and it would be absurd for me to take him on in scientific matters.

However, I am not willing to cede ground to him on the possibilities of a spiritual universe. Just as we cannot fathom infinity in time or space, we cannot know God's purpose in the origin of the universe. Ever to claim such knowledge is just arrogance.

The evolutionary process has been steadily upward, from darkness to light, from rioting vegetation to flowers to poems, from material substance to spirit, from brute existence to self-awareness, to the power of love — God's consciousness ascendent everywhere.

God is majestic beyond our poor power to grasp. His Majesty is revealed in evolutionary patterns which move inexorably to greater complexity, greater elegance, greater beauty, greater love. The dialectical nature of the process is evidenced by the still abounding presence of ancient evil.

I believe that despite the relentless pain and misery of our chaotic world, God is trying to unite us with Himself through Christ.

The Christ event pervades all other future events in the history of humankind. I believe that to live heroically in this world we need to see beyond the appearance of things, get beyond literal interpretation of our sources and the narrowness of our minds, accept our responsibility to confront evil when it appears, yet stay Christ centered.

What does it mean to stay centered on Christ? It means to live with mystery. It means to believe in His mercy, to believe that, having looked at the alternatives, there is nothing more essential than this faith, even when we suffer doubt. Christocentrism means putting Jesus in the very center of the Holy Trinity, understanding that Jesus had to die on the cross to finish his mission of becoming the Christ, all in accordance with God's will. What happened in Christ is how God works to bring about communion with him.

Given endless strife and hatred, it is hard to accept the redemptive example of Jesus. Yet through all this I can see his splendor!

When we look up at the night sky, it seems a peaceful and serene place, yet we know it is anything but that. The universe is a terribly active place, full of creations even more majestic than those we see. Cosmologists estimate that there are 400 billion suns in our galaxy we call the Milky Way and billions of galaxies in the universe, moving invarious directions at tremendous speeds. They speculate on parallel universes, an infinity of possibilities racing, bending and collapsing. We know and speculate on these things by our intelligence and reason. This is the physical universe evolving.

There is also a spiritual one. We know that because of our faith and love, also active, growing and evolving.

There is an eternal process of creation and worship going on, in which men and women throughout the world are engaged acccording to their faith and thought and action. This process is like a dance, a cosmic dance of touch and countertouch, current and countercurrent, a reverberation between us and God, an unending spiritual movement of grace and beauty and purpose flowing out of His immense depths.

XXVIII

Artificial Intelligence and the Singularity I

When I was a professor and dean of the college in the late 1960s, I joined the World Future Society and became an active member. By the late 1970s, I had grown disillusioned with the Society's agenda and dropped out. I thought then that preoccupation with artificial intelligence was a wrongfooted approach to invention of the future. I have since humbly changed my mind. But it was through that association that I first became aware of the significant differences between linear growth and exponential growth.

The lesson of exponential growth is well captured in a description of a lily pond which may grow plants at a seemingly innocent rate, doubling each day until half the pond is covered. The next doubling suddenly covers the entire pond. That is exponential growth. The effect has proven time and again in various activities, such as a bank savings account in which a 21-year-old puts aside $2000 a year, never touches it, and finds a yield of $1 million when he retires at age 65.

The significance of technological change that is now occurring exponentially is outlined by the brilliant computer scientist and forecaster, Raymond Kurzweil, in his "law of accelerating returns". (For an immediate, penetrating description of Kurzweil's work, go to the web and click on *The Singularity Is Near.)*

While most people may be aware of sci-fi depictions of Artificial Intelligence (AI) creations in movies such as Matrix, Terminator, or I Robot (from Isaac Asimov), few are aware of the broader significance of AI in all phases of human endeavor. We are moving on rapidly from narrow AI to Artificial General Intelligence.

Ray Kurzweil and other AI scientists now see the coming of self-aware machines of super intelligence within the next 30 to 40 years, perhaps sooner. This will happen because of the event of Technological Singularity. Kurzweil defines the "Singularity" as a coming epoch, in which the pace of technological change will be so rapid, its impact so deep, that human life will be irreversibly transformed. "Although neither utopian nor dystopian, this epoch will transform the concepts that we rely on to give meaning to our lives, from our business models, to the cycle of human life, including death itself." (KURZWEIL)

Recently, Kurzweil was joined in his prediction of the Singularity by two prominent Artificial Intelligence experts, MIT Professor Patrick Winston, and Jurgen Schmidhuber, Chief Scientist of the company, NNAISENCE.

Schmidhuber states that he is confident that the Singularity "is just 30 years away, if the trend doesn't break, and there will be rather cheap computational devices that have as many connections in your brain, but are much faster. There is no doubt in my mind that AIs are going to become supersmart."

On the fiction side, Richard K.Morgan postulates in his book, "Altered Carbon," in the 25ᵗʰ century, "humankind has spread throughout the galaxy, monitored by the watchful eye of the UN. While division in race, religion, and class still exist, advances in technology have redefined life itself. Now assuming one can afford the expensive procedure, a person's consciousness can be stored in a cortical stack at the base of the brain and easily downloaded into a new body (or "sleeve") making death nothing more than a minor blip on the screen." Remember, this is just science fiction, but interesting to contemplate?

Meanwhile, the phenomenon of accelerating returns continues.We are now beginning to reach the "knee of the exponential curve", which is the stage when the exponential trend quickly becomes explosive, and the curve shoots straight up.

Kurzweil believes that the Singularity will represent "the merger of our biological thinking and existence with our technology, resulting in a world that is still human but transcends our biological roots." He expects thinking machines to pass the "Turing test", meaning that nonbiological intelligence will be indistinguishable from our biological intelligence by 2029. The nonbiological intelligence will be thousands of times more powerful than our unaided intelligence. We shall depend vitally on these thinking machines.(Heavy stuff,isn't it? We shall see.)

What are the implications of such astounding development if it occurs? How shall we learn to live with these machines? Is there much to fear from them, as Asimov's story suggests?

Or in considering the "nano bots" we now hear about regularly, are we in danger of destroying our world by allowing nanotechnology to proceed with the development of these microscopic,self replicating, mechanical structures? Will we lose control of the development of new creation? Is all of this fantastic discovery and invention playing God? What are the possibilities, and consequences, of a "neo Luddite " attempt to halt fantastic technological development? Are Kurzweil and other "singularitarians" wrong in the first place, as some critics argue? These are premier questions for everyone's future.

(Notes: An excellent movie on the mathematical genius, Alan Turing, was made in 2014. Ned Ludd led a worker uprising in late 19th century London to destroy all machines.)

XXIX

Artificial Intelligence and the Singularity II

Throughout my career as an educator, I kept my graduate association with the U.S. Army Artillery School in Oklahoma. During my last visit there, I saw a tall, broad shouldered sergeant walking down the stair, with an artificial leg. I was stunned, and I believe you will see the significance. In conversation with them I learned that he was preparing to go back to Iraq as a functioning squad leader. The prosthetic device he is using is driven by microprocessors at each joint, just one of many new applications that permit amputees who previously would have been unable even to lead normal civilian lives now to return to the battlefield. In one sense the sergeant is a special soldier, yet in a broader context of how our army is developing, he is not extraordinary.

U.S. Army Research, in conjunction with DARPA, is working on a "super warrior," 10 of which would be equivalent to today's brigade. They will have an exoskeleton that allows them to carry 180 pounds as though it were 5 pounds, run and leap like track stars, and will be plugged into a Pentagon grid. Add this new hardware capacity to predator drones. Combine this with new "smart artillery" which is deadly accurate and very fast, yet even these recent developments pale in comparison with the robot army coming.

In this new era, the military robots will have the intelligence to make battlefield decisions that presently belong to humans. They will have significant cognitive advantages over human soldiers. Herein lies the danger that the US Office of Naval Research is now carefully considering.

The perception that robots will only do what humans have programmed them to do falls apart in at least two ways: it fails to take account of artificial intelligence becoming Artificial General Intelligence, and second, that programs are no longer written and understood by a single person. There are teams of programmers, none of whom know the entire program, so no one can predict how large programs will interact without testing in the field, an action unavailable to designers of military robots.

This does not mean that the robots cannot learn a warrior code, just as our human soldiers have done through superb training. But it will be a dramatic undertaking and immensely important to develop the ethical dimension if we are to avoid the peril projected by Asimov in his story, I, *Robot. Can this be done?* Probably, but not certainly. Could we simply stop the development entirely? Perhaps, but not likely.

The dilemma posed here is but one of several to a future of continuing exponential growth—ironically, dilemmas which may depend on nonbiological super intelligence to resolve. The likelihood is that in full maturity, today's kids shall either learn to coexist with subservient robots and conscious machines or face a battle for survival against these super intelligent machines turned psychotic.

But God is with us! Face the existential fact that life is a challenge!

The AI fantasies imagined by science fiction writers have not materialized, at least not yet, but AI is already in more common usage than many people realize. As Nick Bostrom, another AI scientist, has pointed out, AI inspired systems are already integral to many everyday technologies, such as Internet search engines, bank software for processing transactions, software for large inventories, and in medical diagnosis.

My generation has exemplified adaptation to rapid technological change, even those of us who are not technically savvy.(I tell my grandson that I am basically a Luddite.*)*

Consider these developments of the past 50 years: the Personal Computer; communications greatly enhanced by fax machines in the late 1980s;and then by the Internet, invented by US government, but exploited tremendously by entrepreneurs in the private sector. At the same time on the bionic front, I know a man with two artificial knees and two artificial hips;the quality of his life is far beyond what it would have been 50 years ago.

As computers became more powerful, they also became correspondingly less expensive to all, and smaller in the bargain. In the near future they will look like pens that we carry in our pockets. Now it is almost standard that everyone has access to a computer. Of course, there are issues, loss of privacy, for example, but we have learned to adapt and adjust in relatively easy fashion. Our world changed and we changed with it. But there is a dialectic at work here too.We ordinary people did not see much of this coming. We are like passengers facing backwards on a train hurtling with even greater speed into the future.

What my generation has experienced is mild on the growth curve compared with what the next generation shall face. The issues will become much more profound, going to the very heart of what it means to be human. The first question is, can a machine of nonbiological intelligence become self-conscious?

Kurzweil,Bostrum, and other singulartarians are convinced that such an event will happen within the next quarter-century.

If so, how can humans ensure that these super intelligent machines are benevolent allies of humankind? What strategies and policies need to be considered now in order to ensure that the relationships between humans and machines will be positive? What are the prospects for, and the potential consequences, of trans-humanism—the merging of machines and humans in the same entity?

Where is God in the equation for whatever shall evolve?

If we view the dangers as too great to allow continuing technological development, what are our options? Can we stop these trends? I think perhaps we may indeed modify our directions of development in the sense that we have always played a role in our evolution, but that the evidence is too overwhelming contrarily to think that we can, or should, place extreme barriers in the path of science and technology as it seeks to discover how Intelligence is flooding our world.

So far in human history, science and technology have steadily advanced, sometimes with quantum leaps. Science has a natural overarching capability to go around irrational obstacles. The long-term trend of technological innovation is perpetual advancement.

As Ray Kurzweil says, *"Only technology can provide the scale to overcome the challenges with which society struggled for generations. Emerging technologies will provide the means of providing and storing clean and renewable energy, removing toxins and pathogens from our bodies and the environment, and providing the knowledge and wealth to overcome hunger and poverty."*

It is an awesome challenge. If there are moments when the load becomes too much to bear, *"Choose something like a star... to stay the mind upon."*(Robert Frost)

XXX

Artificial Intelligence and the Singularity III

When the Singularity comes, as I believe it will, another great leap in the evolutionary process will change our world in a manner similar to the human species becoming self-aware eons ago. When that was exactly we cannot know, but it was then that God created us in His image, not physically but spiritually, with a capacity for moral choice and creative design.

Whether or not our new self-aware creations, *thinking machines,* will have a soul is a subject of debate in the community of artificial intelligence scientists. The level of intelligence they will bring is also debatable, but most projections place it much higher than our own. There is an important difference between our evolution and their's: we did not create ourselves, but we are the agents creating these machines, at least until such time as they supersede us in their replication. In this sense we are a partner in the evolutionary process.

With the emergence of the human soul, there is a different kind of deity which begins to express itself, not to spare humankind from the "problem of evil," but to provide guidance, compassion, and the healing power of love. In our conscience and experience we can find the highest, noblest expression of this love. In the words of St. John, *"The word was made flesh, and dwelt among us, and we beheld his glory, the glory of the only begotten of the Father, full of grace and truth."*

I agree with those who contend that this belief can only be taken on faith. There is a distinction between God as Creator and God as Love. The mystery of the difference between physical evolution and spiritual evolution is magnified by its receding dialectical nature and the upending unity of all forces, "the all in all of Christ."

On what basis can we believe these things? Is it science, or religion, or philosophy? I contend for, and urge readers to think seriously about, a new ground being formed which authentically combines science and faith in the invention of the new world through artificial intelligence. Faith in a loving God left out of the equation for guidance and wisdom is an omission potentially devastating.

<u>Expand the term to Artificial General Intelligence</u>. Artificial intelligence has been with us for more than four decades in ways we now take for granted. But when you have an AI system that can assist in the design of improved versions of itself, you could go overnight to something radically super intelligent.(See Bostrom)

Unity is our watchword in dealing with Artificial General Intelligence, unity of human beings and super intelligent machines. I am not thinking of trans-humanism here, although some AI experts like Kurzweil envision that kind of development, but obviously our challenge as creators will be to help ensure that ultimate loyalty is structured into the "soul" of these machines, not simply as an Asimov rule, but as part of a mutually held moral and ethical consciousness given to us by God.

Can a machine understand its human organs, its history? Even more charismatic, can a machine become aware of God's presence? It remains to be seen, but there are reasons to believe that, aided by super intelligence, humankind may reach a higher ground spiritually and materially than we have ever known before. The opposite would surely be <u>the end of days.</u>

End Notes

What are your personal beliefs? I believe in the Holy Trinity. I believe in the institutions of marriage and family. I believe in the U.S. Constitution and the Bill of Rights. I believe in protecting women and children and the environment. I believe that truth ultimately wins out over lies.

Is there anything else you believe? If you want to play around, here's a list possibly to consider:

I believe there's no business like show business, and nothing like a Dame, prosperity is just around the corner, the only thing we have to fear is fear itself, this generation has a rendezvous with destiny, when more and more people are thrown out of work unemployment results, necessity is the mother of invention, the Iceman cometh, the postman always rings twice, and Kilroy was here.

Face the music: Illecitimus non carborundum!

I believe in miracles, and that only God can make a tree, and there will be bluebirds over the white cliffs of Dover tomorrow when the world is free, and that anyone who goes to a psychiatrist ought to have his head examined.

I would rather be right then be president, and I would rather see a purple cow then be one.

Don't shoot the messenger, and don't give up the ship, and don't tread on me.

Go and do the right thing, with love.

****

Rich Lowry's article, "Considering Our Fracking Future, " 7/10/13, reveals with rich irony the Orwellian methods of "journalists," like Lowry, to dissuade us from finding the truth. Orwellian interpretations of what's going on abound, and are astonishingly successful in disarming people. It could be said more simply that these are lies, but that misses the process of how it's done. Press and government agents do not tell lies; after all, they have a responsibility to clarify events and provide more nuanced explanations. Some shape of the truth still exists. Thus, we are suborned and more careful about drawing critical conclusions because we want to believe in our government and in a free and responsible press.

Here's a key question: what should be the highest priority of our government— citizen rights to protection? or business proprietary rights? The question was answered in 2005 when the Safe Drinking Water Act was amended to exempt fracking.

The American leaders I admire most are Abraham Lincoln, George Washington, Robert E. Lee, John Muir, Martin Luther King Jr, and the great Lakota Chief, Tashunko Witco (Crazy Horse). But I also admire Great Britain's Prime Minister, Winston Churchill, whom I consider to be the greatest man of the 20th century.

The greatest of the English speaking poets were Robert Burns, a Scotsman, William Butler Yeats, an Irishman, Dylan Thomas, a Welshman, Emily Dickinson and Robert Frost, American, Rainer Maria Rilke, a German, and Alfred Lord Tennyson, an Englishman (oh well, one is better than none.)

Ben Johnson and the man from Stratford:" No, Ben, it's all nothing. We come, we go, and when were done we're done... When he talks like that, there's nothing for a man to do, but lead him somewhere for a drink."

Yeats said it, "the worst thing about some men is that when they are not drunk they are sober." Reminds me of Churchill at a party when he was drunk and argued with a lady. Churchill lost his cool and said "Madam,you are just ugly." She immediately replied, "you, sir, are drunk!" He replied just as quick, "yes, you're right about that, but I will be sober in the morning."

My favorite athletes were Stan Musial, Ted Williams, Johnny Unitas, Joe Montana, Bobby Orr, Gil Perrault, Steve Nash, Cal Ripken, Mariano Rivera, Derek Jeter, Peyton Manning. I liked the St. Louis Cardinals when I was young, and the New York Yankees when I was old.

****

A wild bird, tossed into flight of no beginning and uncertain end, some time belief suspended but ultimately steady in faith and flight, admits his errors and sins on this earth before a loving God; as for those who were loved, or were wronged, he cannot tell you now; when the winds drive and whirl and blow him along no longer, maybe then, some better time.

I look for the heavenly Elysian fields, the solitude and elegance of reconciliation.

JOH: 3/1/18 Cursom Perficio

Acknowledgements

I remain indebted to sources and citations listed in my previous iUniverse books, *Reading Yeats and Striving to Be a College President, and Chasing Crazy Horse I and II*, especially the following:

Alan Bloom, *the closing of the American mind: how higher education has failed democracy and impoverished the soles of today's students*, Simon and Schuster, 1987

Diane Ravitch, *the language police*, Alfred A Knopf, 2003

Jerry L Martin and Anne D.Neil, *defending civilization: how our universities are failing America and what can be done about it*, American Council of Trustees and Alumni, 2002

Ray Kurzweil, *the singularity is near,* Penguin Books, 2005

J. Storrs Hall, *beyond AI*, Prometheus Books, 2007

Stephen W. Hawking, a brief history of time, Bantam Books, 1988

John O. Hunter, *For the Love of Poetry*, Amazon Create Space, 2009

George F. Kennan, around the cragged hill, W. W. Norton, 1993

Nicholas Berdyaev, the origin of Russian Communism, translated by RM French,

Ann Arbor paperback, 1960 (first published in 1937)

Alexander Solzhenitsyn, the Gulag Archipelago, translated by Thomas P. Whitney and Harry Willits, HarperCollins, 1985

Solzhenitsyn, "One Word of Truth", Nobel Lecture, translated by Nicholas Bethel, Sten Valley Press, London, 1970

Asar Nafisi, reading Lolita in Tehran, Random House, 2003

John W. Kiser, the monks of Tibhirinne, St. Martin's Griffin, 2002

John Preble, the Highland clearances, Penguin Books, 1963

Theodore Dalrymple, our culture, what's left of it, Ivan R.Dee, 2005

Immanuel Kant, religion within limits of reason, in the philosophy of Kant, by Carl J Friedrich, Random House, 1949

John Paul II, rise and let us be on our way, Warner Books, 2004

John Paul II, crossing the threshold of hope, Alfred A.Knopf, 1994

George Weigel, the cube and the cathedral, Basic Books, 2005

Michael H. Murray, the thought of Teilhard de Chardin, Seabury Press, 1966

Ernest Becker, the structure of evil, Free Press, 1968

Victor Frankl, the search for meaning, Beacon Press, 2006 (first published, 1946)

Robert Littell, the Stalin epigram, Simon and Schuster, 2009

Richard J Finnerman,Ed, <u>the Yeats reader, revised edition</u>, Scribner, 1997

William Butler Yeats, <u>mythologies,</u> Simon and Schuster, 1959

P. Hateley Waddell, <u>the life and poems of Robert Burns,</u> David Wilson, Glasgow, 1867

<u>a critique of the poems of Robert Burns</u>, printed by John Brown, 1812

Also, for this work, the following:

Robert Louis Wilken, "Christianity Face to Face with Islam<u>", First Things</u>, 2010

Dean Miller, *Deep State*,American Survivor,2017

I am especially indebted to Amazon Audible Books for the following:

Jack Weatherford,*Genghis Khan and the Making of the Modern World*,Amazon Audible Bookl

Yuval Noah Harari, *sapiens, A History of Humankind*, Amazon Audible Book

Yuval Noah Harari, *Homo Deus*, Amazon Audible Book

George Orwell, *1984, New Classical Edition*, Amazon Audible Book

Pierre Teilhard de Chardin, *The Divine Milieu*, Amazon Kindle Edition

Jordan B. Peterson, *12 Rules for Life: Antidote for Chaos,* YouTube

Lettters and Articles from Judicial Watch

Ancient Christian Wisdom, files, Word Press.com, 2014

END OF DAYS?

Part Two

Stepping Wildly Into Theology

Table of Contents Part Two

Intro: A Personal Note

During my college presidencies in the late 80s and 90s, my avocation involved study in philosophy and religion. I am immensely grateful for my time spent at St. Bonaventure University, where I enrolled in theology courses;at Oxford University where I participated in the Oxford Round Table and enjoyed a summer on the Thames River; at Harvard University, where I spent my leave of absence; and at the Abbey of Genesee, where through many retreats, I became introduced to monastic life, and found the wonderful tapes of Thomas Merton, Novice Master at Gethseme Abbey,Kentucky.

These institutions provided for me not only rich sources for academic study, but they were wonderful places of peace and spiritual contemplation. For the most part, I have been a lone ranger in my searches but I am deeply indebted to many sources, such as those listed above, and for the galvanizing opportunities on my long, sometimes erratic road to conversion. I thank God for His blessings on this road-- for His lovingkindness, healing power, and forgiveness.

Any errors or mistakes in this book are mine alone. JOH

Chapter I
The Splendor of Truth

This year of 2018 marks the 25th anniversary of John Paul II's encyclical on the splendor of truth. Although Christianity is under attack in many ways, we may be grateful that in the 20th century we had such leaders as John Paul II, Alexander Solzhenitsyn, Vaclav Havel, and Martin Luther King Jr. to remind us of our roots and keep a steady on a path to defeat the lie, reminding us that truth must sit in the highest chair. We are still suffering the will of the last century that have not yet been healed in our public discourse, political institutions, and popular culture. Yet, praise to God, we can be grateful to these Christian champions for their steadfast leadership.

In his encyclical, *Veritatus Splendor,* John Paul clarified again that truth exists in spite of all the ideological warfare and demonic efforts to purge it. Though the search is sometimes a thicket of difficulty, the truth can be found. We don't create truth, we find it, and we have no power to change it. The truth may not make us comfortable, but it does make us free. Knowing and living the truth saves our souls, and it is the only path to lasting happiness.

As I have moved into God's wilderness, I see more clearly absolutes beneath the relative. Is it possible that the essence of my belief in a personal God who brings us love and truth may be strengthened by a search for any shared experience or values among different religions? In this search, we must accept that we are limited. From a Christian point of view, it is faith, not knowledge, that leads to salvation. But I believe God is always with us in efforts to find His truth.

If there is anything not true in my religious beliefs, I wish to discard it. If there is anything true that I may gain from exploring other religions, I wish to embrace it, for God is truth and love and beauty.

****

Chapter II
Exploring Paul's Charisma

This is a personal reflection on Paul's charisma with reference to Jesus. In trying to arrive at a better understanding of how Paul became so dominant, or at least frame good questions about him, I need to assert that I do not claim any authority as a theologian. I am indebted to several theologians whom I will credit in my endnotes.

If, as Paul taught, we are "all one in Jesus Christ" (*Galatian*s 3:28), there must be a theological underpinning for a comparison of Paul and Jesus,although the comparison may be more difficult than some Christians would believe. I admit, however, that I am not so concerned about theological correctness as about raising questions that may be "out of grace," i.e. too intellectual to really matter except that they are interesting to me, and therefore I feel the need to keep Jesus in the picture as reference and divine guide. My approach to theological investigation is founded on the desire to surrender to the mystery of Christian faith.

The questions are definitely loaded against my ability and insight: For example, what inspired Paul's early ardor against the church? Was that quality of mind transferred intact after his conversion? Or was his zeal transformed in some way beyond an acceptance of Jesus as Christ? Was his vision on the road to Damascus his moment of conversion? If so, why does he spend so little detail on it other than in connection with his apostolic authority? How long was he in Damascus after his Revelation experience, and what did he go through at that time? How did his thought develop during the long period prior to his journeys?

If the appearance of Jesus to Paul was not physical (assuredly, authentically spiritual), why does he accept other experiences as physical, if they are not a cultural dictate? How deep and constant was his conflict personally with Peter? Did Peter accept his admonishment (*Galatians 2*:14)? Did Paul always think of himself as a Jew, even if suspect and under attack by Jews? Ultimately, is it fair to say that he founded the Christian religion?

What does Paul mean when he says that we are "all in Christ?" What is meant by Christ as "all in all?"

In *Galatians*, Paul probes and attacks relentlessly, as a man who seems to be fighting for his authority and integrity. He sees enemies. Much seems taken for granted in the understanding of what was said and done that provoked Paul; is it lost to us?

Consider his arguments to the Galatians: *"There are some who trouble you." (1:17) "If someone is preaching to you a gospel contrary to that which you received, let him be accursed."(1:9) "Who hindered you from obeying the truth?" (5:7) " I wish those who unsettle you would mutilate themselves."(5:12) "Henceforth, let no man trouble me, for I bear on my body the marks of Jesus."(6:17)"*

It's very interesting that in these chapters Paul refers to these enemies and denounces them in the strongest terms. We see here how far from the example of Jesus are his personality and approach.

Let us assume the timeless nature of human politics, what ever the substance of the issues. So close are we to an identification of these enemies and illumination of the political environment, yet Paul does not name them. Why not? Is it possible that he really does not know them? Yet, what explains that he would not know them,given the combined power of his attack and the theology he was inspired to deliver?

If he really did not know his enemies, then truly we stand in awe of such a glorious anger. Where did it come from? It is easy to conclude that the Spirit was at work, but perhaps another explanation is that he did not know his enemies and ingeniously used constructive ambiguity. In other words, he was acutely aware of the need to contain his anger for political reasons while unleashing it fully and furiously in service of the Gospel. (See Duncan)

"For through the law I died to the law, that I might live for God. I have been crucified with Christ, it is no longer I who live, but Christ who lives in me."(Galatians 2:19) Paul knows the wisdom of paradox.

Also interesting to note is that Paul's references are usually to Christ Jesus or Jesus Christ, sometimes to our Lord Jesus Christ, less frequently to Jesus. *Vine's Expository Dictionary* explains the various uses in Paul's epistles: "Christ Jesus" describes the exalted one who emptied himself and testifies to his preexistence; "Jesus Christ"describes the despised and rejected one who was afterward glorified. "Christ Jesus" suggests his grace; "Jesus Christ" suggests his glory.

Does Paul's own spiritual understanding and guidance make unnecessary references to the personal life and example of Jesus? Would the church have evolved differently if Paul had made more room for Jesus prior to the cross in his explication of Christ? Or did it all simply unfold as God willed and wills it?

Does not Paul's own charisma account for his approach to Jesus? Paul saw the world as a battlefield. His perspective on this world follows from a spirituality of crisis and salvation. It is secure in God's love but alert and combative and daring.

In contrast, the ministry of Jesus showed him to be the *Prince of Peace.* Whereas Paul was dogmatic and harsh, Jesus was warm, patient, loving, noncombatant, unpretentious, flexible, secure not only in his Father's love but in his own authority. His splendor exceeded Paul's.

Jesus taught about the kingdom of God. Paul taught about Christ. Paul recognized, of course, the suffering of Jesus on the cross. He connected his own life to the death of Jesus, imitating Jesus' example on the cross and sharing with him God's redemptive plan.Paul says in *Ist Corinthians,* *"when reviled, we bless, when persecuted, we* endure."

In my perhaps superficial way, I see the connection between Jesus and Paul as uncertain. Paul's way of thinking is different, yet truly, he is bound to Jesus. Except for Jesus, Paul is easily a cut above all other figures of the New Testament. His charisma is explained in that, like Jesus, his spiritual insight was so deep that he went beyond any personality or personage-- even that of Jesus?

According to Max Weber, who coined the term, *Charisma, it stands for a particular kind of authority that rests on devotion to the exceptional sanctity, heroism or exemplary character of an individual person.* (See Weber, *Bureaucracy.*)

*Weber contends that Charism*a is not an individual trait but a social phenomenon, dependent on a group of believers. This was the way for Paul, who won over not only the early Gentile Christians but became more and more fixed in the Christian canon. He was overwhelming. Peter did not have this effect even though he too, of course, has a permanent place in Christianity.

It seems clear that Paul did not depend on the historical Jesus for answers to the questions bombarding the newfound faith of Jesus as Savior.

It may be dangerous to speculate too much on mystery, but it seems essential to come to terms with the mystical connotations of being united in Christ. We rely on the doctrine of the Trinity. In contemporary terms, we come <u>to</u> God the Father (unknowable) <u>through</u> Jesus Christ, <u>in</u> the Spirit.

"Clear knowledge is not necessary." (Thomas Merton)

Registering my own conclusions, I need to acknowledge that for me a problem with theology is that it is possible to become confused by it, and so I admit that I have invaded wildly into this field. I do so in the hope that it opens new possibilities of truth. I remain unclear and continually intrigued about Christ as the "all in all."

I admire Paul's charisma. I like both his mysticism and his certitude. He was, I believe, as close to God as any man could ever be.

I hear Paul saying that God the Father, unknown and inscrutable, out of love for His creation gave definition to Himself through His son, Jesus Christ. We may not know the Father but we do know Christ. Paul speaks of Christ and the Holy Spirit as one and the same, and he speaks of a time when Christ will be the "all in all." All of this is very meaningful, restorative and enhancing.

My faith, however, is built on the revelation of God through history. I accept the orthodoxy of the Christian Trinity, in all of its mystery, even as I question and open myself to new possibilities. My prayer continues: Praise Father, Son, and Holy Spirit, the God who is, who was, and is to come, at the end of the ages.

****

Chapter III
Developing Communities of Love and Service

During my career as a college president, I borrowed as much as I could from the field of organization development. If I had not been president with myriad other duties and interests, I would have focused my work on contributing to this field.

Let's begin here with an article of faith: *communities of love and service will grow if they are truly Christ centered.*

Yet, even within genuinely committed churches, factions emerge which lead to strife and disintegration and even alienation. Even those who love, or say they love, may tear at the body of Christ. Given the increasing diversity of our society and multicultural trends, the challenge to integrate in the name and love of Christ becomes even more complex.

Human knowledge has gained from the social sciences, but the reality of God is not comprehended by them.. Yet we may be grateful that there are different forms of knowledge, different ways of knowing, which are not necessarily irreconcilable.

Every community is culturally bound and limited historically,certainly true of Christian communities,but in setting up a framework for an Organization Development (OD) approach we need to go further than acknowledgement of standard discipline results.

Christianity has tended to be ignorant of other worldviews and to develop exclusively: i.e., only we Christians have truth and everyone else is in error. An <u>inclusive approach </u>would recognize that truth may be found everywhere even as we recognize that we have the fullest truth. In other words, if there is anything in any other religion that is true, it is of God and therefore belongs to the Christian as well.

The tendency is to ignore the growth possibilities of venture community dialogue or to distrust it as potentially polluting. This was not true of the earliest Christian communities, as clearly evidenced in St. Paul's work, but real dialogue probably had ceased by the end of the second century. The obvious distinction is between dialogue for rapprochement or proselytization for religious advancement.

<u>Inclusive vision </u>is marked in organization development technique because of its transdisciplinary character: It is flexible and resilient in exploration of goals setting and evaluation, resource development, conflict resolution, communication methods, cultural and environmental problems, human motivational factors, administrative structure, power and authority – – all of which are useful for community development. Organization development is also a field of pragmatic interests: what works?

The social sciences on which organization development is grounded do not perceive very well the religious sensibilities of men and women in organizational life, despite millions of people in the world who are religious, and despite much evidence that religious explanations are as readily tolerated as scientific explanations for the same data. The lack of a religious perspective impedes a full analysis of the phenomenon which are the subjects of social sciences.

We come full circle: I am not suggesting that militant answers to the problems of religious community development will be found, only that we may be advanced in our search through organization development technique.

What is a community?

Community is the opposite of alienation, aloneness, non-alliance, impersonal action. Community descriptors are needs and goals, integration, trust, openness, togetherness, identity, mutual respect and sharing. Communities of various types are constantly struggling to be born. While the senses of integrity and alliance are imbued in the notion of a community, individuals do not identify with one community exclusively.

Thus a religious community may form alongside a political community within the same geographical area. Given the challenge of ethnic and cultural diversity, special attention is needed to the idea of <u>plural community</u>:

As Robert Nisbet said, it derives the all-important idea of *communitas communitatum*. In other words, it serves the idea that diversity, autonomy and decentralization are possible for local communities, coexisting within the larger community. As a philosophical concept, <u>*community*</u> does not necessarily imply localism, though as Nisbet also pointed out, localism is a strong element in the notion of a pluralistic community.(See note on Robert Nisbet.)

Let's assume that a religious community, serving more important moral and ethical ideas, may fit within a pluralistic context. What then are the motivational strategies and techniques which will allow this to happen?

In the following treatment, a three dimensional approach is taken: *community development is first seen as a matter of fostering organizational health, then as a continuing problem of conflict resolution; and finally and more broadly, as a recognition of transformational principles of growth in which community is identified with nature and the vast scheme of God's creation.*

Organizational Health

All communities are organized in some fashion, even those which purposefully avoid bureaucratic structure.All require some kind of organization to address needs and problems and make decisions. A primary question is, how healthy is the organization?

The treatment of organizational health in secular technocratic society draws heavily on human behavior theories. Two exemplars are Douglas McGregor and Abraham Maslow. McGregor echoes Maslow's descriptions of the hierarchy of needs, and proceeds from this line of humanistic interpretation based essentially on an opposite set of assumptions. It's dialectical.

Work may be a source of satisfaction: creativity, self direction, and sense of responsibility are natural in most people. Since self-motivation is a strong innate potential, waiting to be released, the task of leadership is to build commitment by properly challenging the abilities and interests of people within the organization.Effective integration demands that both the organization's needs and the individual needs be recognized in any decision making process, and further, that the individual should be an active participant in the total needs assessment.

Facing realistically the problem of integrating the individual and the organization needs, conflict resolution is essential. It is a mistake to confuse organization health with ideals such as harmony, happiness and contentment, important though these may be in other contexts. Simply by the nature of organization, tension and conflict are bound to exist. Maslow said, conflict is of course a sign of relative health,as you would know if you ever met really apathetic people, people who have given up hoping, striving and coping.(See Maslow.)

****

Chapter IV

In Organization Development, there are numerous methods for resolving conflict, but four seem to predominate: <u>mediation, arbitration, compromise, and reconciliation.</u> In arbitration, after hearing all parties and weighing the evidence, a decision is made. In compromise, all parties relinquish something in order to move off dead center. In reconciliation, the parties are joining so that the same value positions are held by all.

The highest form of mediation (or ministry) would resolve the conflict not only by reconciling the parties but in such a way that the result contributes to community development.

In the social sciences, there is much said about the quality of life and the need to bring technology under the service of the seemingly all-inclusive concept, but without reference to the Creator's purpose.

Social scientists have failed to see unifying principles in God's involvement in human and natural development. They have not seen, for example, that social organizations may be growth oriented in the same way as biological organisms are. Indeed the whole world may be alive.

There is nothing new about holism and transformational theory. Teilhard de Chardin developed the seams. Another contribution was made by George Land, *Grow or Die: The Unifying Principle of Transformation.*

In describing the unifying principle of transformation, Land presented the thesis that all life forms share the same behavioral processes. These processes are focused on growth. Growth is defined as continual joining of larger amounts of information (energy) into meaningful relationships, and an organized form.

There are three types of growth: 1) *accretive* -- enlargement of the total organism which is merely additive and identical; 2) *replicative* -- growth through generation of other like organisms in which the growth of each organism is reinforced;3) *mutualistic* -- growth through symbiotic relationships, which even though complex, are characterized by a high degree of cooperation between different organizations attracted to each other for mutual growth support. All systems tend to evolve by progressing from one level to the next, always as a result of environmental interactions and relations.

Through a series of examples, Land demonstrated growth in psychological and social systems as well as in physical and biological systems through the same principles. The conclusion is that living processes are *ubiquitous and universal: "Transformation maintains that psychological and cultural processes are an extension of and are isomorphic with biological, physical and chemical processes."* (Land)

How does this work further our understanding of organization and community development? What helps directly is the application of transformational principles in a circumscribed area. Land explains community growth as most healthful when it has achieved a stage of mutualism -- that is, when it is accompanied by the growth of communication patterns, good support systems, relationships with other communities, etc.

The community as an organism remains autonomous but not isolated. When the continued physical growth occurs, however, as a new form of accretive, a pathological state may be created in which the community functions break down under too much pressure.

Important to recognize is that principles of adaptation as well as of growth are endemic in the transformational process. The relationships between any system and its environment are dynamically worked out as the system strives to fit itself well into its environment and to make the environment fit its needs at the same time.

Communities either grow and adapt or die. So we return to the idea of a religious community providing moral forces and stability through Christian love and service, coexisting with other communities in a diverse, pluralistic, even "multi- cultural" society.

That there are transformational principles which may be used to analyze community development is another indication of God's purpose and pattern in his creation.

****

Chapter V
Christians and the Question of Historical Guilt

"Martin Luther King Jr. is dead. He was killed by a white man's bullet."

Think back for a moment; when you first heard these words, what were your genuine thoughts and feelings? Did you feel guilty about his assassination? Should white people in our society feel guilty in general about the crimes committed against our black brothers and sisters?

My first reaction to the news of King's death was a mix of sadness and excitement. It was similar to that which occurred to me when I first heard the news of Pres. Kennedy's assassination: what will be the effect on the country? I must confess, however, that I did not feel guilt. There were no pangs of conscience. But this was an initial reaction, which may not be the true experience. Every genuine human experience has a form and pattern, the first step of which is merely preliminary to the total definition of it.

As a responsible citizen of white American society, should I feel guilty about the death of Martin Luther King?. Is there such a thing as collective guilt, a guilt imposed by which we live?

My viewpoint expressed here must draw upon my historical understanding and what, for lack of a better term, might be called a "philosophy of history." For the latter, I owe much to a Spanish philosopher, José Ortega y Gasset.

It should be clear to all of us that America is a violent society: violence has always been close to the surface in our way of life. We have the highest crime rate of any society; our cities are seething with racial turmoil and hostility. In this land of affluence and democratic achievement, how did we get this way? It's impossible to account for all of the factors, of course, but we can single out one.

At the birth of our nation, we injected into history a great promise, a dream to be fulfilled. We laid down a philosophical foundation of individual freedom, justice under the law, and equality for all men. These are not merely technical or economic propositions. They are thoroughly moral considerations. Like it or not, these are the ideals by which our civilization shall be judged. To ignore them is an attempt to ignore history itself, perhaps even to join in the absurd fantasy to eradicate history.

Throughout American history we have striven through the process of democratic reform to sustain and fulfill these ideals, but there has been since the beginning one disjointed reality that has always threatened to become our fatal flaw. When these words, *"all men are created equal"*, were being established for posterity, America was at the same time attempting to justify slavery. Equality and slavery are irreconcilable opposites.

We were not the only people caught in the bind, but slavery was America's "peculiar institution"--peculiar because America's slaves in a free white society were of the Negro race. Or all the proud words about America, the "melting pot society," the crippling influence of race has always been strong.

Beyond that however, slavery was America's peculiar institution because of the way in which it was practiced. Until recently, it was difficult to find in our history books true accounts of the human suffering that marked America's institutions of slavery.

In Latin America, slaves had rights protecting them against many specific abuses from their masters. The power to inflict certain physical punishments upon slaves was limited by law, and slaves could obtain legal redress if the master overstepped his bounds. Married slaves could not be separated from each other against their will. The children followed the status of their mother and the child of a free mother remained free even if she later became a slave.

By contrast, in the USA, the slave had practically no protection by law from the arbitrary exercise of authority by the master. The slave had no property rights. Married partners could be separated from each other, and children from their parents. That they were sold is attested to in a large number of advertisements, of which the following is typical:

"Negroes for sale. A Negro woman, 24 years of age, and her two children; said Negroes will be sold separately, or together, as desired. The woman is a good seamstress. She will be sold low for cash, or exchanged for groceries....." (See Marden and Meyer, pp.222-223)

In Latin America, there was a steady change from slavery to freedom going on all the time. In the United States, slavery grew steadily stronger until in 1857 it was given the sanction of the Supreme Court itself. The climax came in the words of Chief Justice Taney, who in his famous decision in the Dred Scott case declared," A Negro has no rights which a white man need respect." Despite the words of the U.S. Constitution, the Negro was branded inferior, "altogether unfit to associate with the white race." On July 4th of that same year, Americans celebrated again the signing of the Declaration of Independence which gave to us and the world those immortal words,*"all men are created equal."*

The fact that slavery grew so strong in the early 19th century on the basis of the myth of racial inferiority is an important historical factor. It does much to explain why the 13th amendment, which freed slaves in the legal sense after the Civil War, did not protect them from the caste barriers that were erected in both North and South. (See Marden and Meyer)

The resort to violence through secret societies, such as the Ku Klux Klan, came about naturally. WJ Cash, a southern historian, said that in this period and after thousands of blacks were murdered by the lynch mob. We know this to be true historically. The murder of three civil rights workers in Mississippi in 1964 was unusual and notable only because two of the three were white.

<u>Two black leaders take on white society</u>

What have been the costs of this history of racial violence and discrimination? It's accurate but too easy to say that it has poisoned our society. The discrimination has obviously led to much despair. By no means a compensating factor, it is also true that this despair can turn an outstanding individual into a paragon of hostility brilliantly conceived. Here I want to recount one of the most marvelous personal stories I have ever read, contained in his Autobiography:

It's about a black man who attended a white school in Lansing Michigan as a boy. He must have been a bright and attractive boy, for he was at the top of his class and was elected class president in the seventh grade then one day an incident occurred that must be familiar to thousands of black kids. His English teacher told him that he ought to begin thinking about his career. The boy said that he would like to be a lawyer. His teacher suggested carpentry instead. "We all here like you, you know that, the teacher said,but you've got to be realistic about being a Nigger."

The boy left Lansing deeply alienated. In the slums of Boston and New York he became a "hustler," selling numbers, women and dope. He said in his autobiography," all of us who might have probed space or cured cancer or built industries, where instead we were black victims of the white man's American social system." We know now that this was an exaggeration; there were many Blacks who rose above the poverty and discrimination and became successful.

But for this young man it was no exaggeration. Had he been entirely white, instead of irretrievably "Negro," he might easily have become a leader of the bar. In his underworld, he went from marijuana to cocaine. To meet the cost he took up burglary. He was arrested with a white mistress who had become his lookout woman. In 1946, not not quite 21, he was sentenced to 10 years in prison. In prison he made a desperate effort to replace the drugs. He was a vicious prisoner, often in solitary; the other prisoners nicknamed him " Satan".

But this prison had on unusually well stacked library to which he was introduced by a fellow prisoner. Prison became his university. There also he was converted to the nation of Islam.

The important word here is <u>conversion.</u> As William James said in his writings on religious experience, "*Were we writing the history of the mind from the purely natural history point of view, we would still have to write down man's liability to sudden and complete conversions as one of his most curious peculiarities.*"

The conversion in this black man's case was complete, as strong as the story of any Christian hero. He went from despair to elation. He had been *born again,* and now for the first time he began to release the leadership and drive and brilliance that were latent in him. They were directed against white American society. He had been converted to a new life, but that life was totally alienated from white America. He began to write and speak brilliantly.

In simple imagery, savagely uncompromising, he drove home the real truth about the Negro's position in America: " Those hunkies that just got off the boat," he said in one of his favorite comparisons, "they are already Americans: Polacks are already Americans; the Italian refugees are already Americans; everything that comes out of Europe, every blue-eyed thing, is already an American; but as long as you and I have been over here we aren't Americans yet. And they don't have to pass civil rights legislation to make a Polack American."

He counseled violence, but he defended this as an answer to white violence. " If they make the klan nonviolent, I'll be nonviolent ... If he only understands the language of a rifle, get a rifle. If he only underands the language of a rope, get a rope. But don't waste time talking the wrong language to a man if you really want to communicate with him."

This man was killed by black assassins in 1965. His name was Malcolm X. What makes his life such a moving a story was his great capacity to learn and to grow, the first quality of a leader. From the time of his conversion to his death, he was constantly searching for new ideas. I believe in time he would have become a leader whom both black and white people would have respected, but he and we were not given that opportunity.

In this attempt to render as clearly as I can black experience in a white culture (remember, I am white), so far I have stressed the theme of violence. The question of guilt confronting us is not reducible to a simple accounting of the dark side of American history. There is conflict in our society precisely because the ideals of freedom and equality have given rise to democratic institutions.

We have changed. We have made progress in turning these ideals into reality. The sharp rise of expectations among our exploited minority groups is in large measure the result of the progress that has been made. Our federal government is not following an apartheid policy. Since the 1950s, all three branches – – executive, legislative, and judicial – – have taken concrete, dramatic steps to resolve the racial crisis.

But government does not control history, and cannot overcome the legacy of history simply by passing new laws. America's racial crisis is essentially a moral problem that requires for its amelioration massive exertion of will by the people and an inspired leadership to set new directions for our culture. This was the role played by Martin Luther King.

King knew America's sickness. He recognized that the society was struggling to cure itself, and he was a minister in that struggle. A day or so after his death, one of our local newspapers carried an advertisement that read something like this: *"At this time of their mourning, we would like to extend our sympathy to the Negro community for the tragic death of Martin Luther King."* No doubt, it was a sincere gesture, but how blind!

It is wrong to say that Martin Luther King was a champion of black Americans. He was much more than that. Malcolm X. was a champion of black America, but King was trying to save the whole of America. He was our contemporary apostle of the American dream *:" I have a dream that my four little children will one day live in a nation where they will not be judged by the color of their skin but by the content of their character."*

King preached nonviolence. He clearly saw that no solution to America's racial problems lies in the direction of force and extremism. In his person and leadership he was squarely in the Enlightenment tradition of democratic reform.

Now finally we come to the bottom-line question: are we guilty as members of a violent society for his death? History can teach us that we are. Indeed historical understanding leads up to the knowledge that what we have done is what we are.

But we must recognize, before we convict ourselves, that we have been and are many things. It's difficult to draw up a balance sheet. We must also distinguish between society and the individual; society is not a mere collection of individuals. In the concept of collective guilt there is a built-in excuse for all the evils that afflict us. The concept of collective guilt does not make us more responsible human beings; on the contrary it can mean an end to personal responsibility. If we are all guilty, then we are, none of us responsible.

With the deaths of of Malcolm X. and Martin Luther King Jr., I believe we can know the meaning of the words of John Donne:

"Any man's death diminishes me, because I am involved in mankind, and therefore never send to know for whom the Bell tolls; it tolls for thee."

Most importantly, I believe this is a deeply Christian persuasion.

I agree with those who argue that America is at another turning point in its history. "Black lives matter" is real. What are the chances that we shall continue to explore the Christian path, led by the example of Jesus Christ? In today's world it is easy to be a pessimist, but I believe that in Christianity the odds are with us, not against us.

I close with a passage from Thomas Wolfe's *You Can't Go Home Again.* Including Martin Luther King, it is a statement that many great Christian leaders and artists would approve:

"I believe that we are lost here in America, but I believe we shall be found. And this belief, which mounts now to the catharsis of knowledge and conviction, is for me, and I think for all of us, not only our hope, but America's everlasting, living dream. I think that true discovery of our own democracy is still before us. I think I speak for most men(and women) living when I say that our America is Here, is Now, and beckons on before us."

I accept and mutualize Wolfe's statement not simply because it echoes other Christian leaders, but because foremost it is in accord with the teaching of Jesus Christ.

****

Chapter VI
Buddha and Eastern Religions

In *Religious Worlds,* William E. Paden declares that " *Religious systems are more effectively understood as worlds rather than as beliefs... The study of religion is not limited to analyzing historical traditions but also investigates the religious language common to all traditions, the language of myth, God, ritual and sacrifice – – in short, the language of the sacred.*"

Sixth century B.C.

It's very interesting that three great teachers and founders of Eastern religions -- Mahavira, Confucius, and Siddharta Gautama (Buddha) were contemporaries of the sixth century BC. The legendary Lao Tzu, associated with Taoism, is also thought to have lived during this period. It's also important to note that Hindu thought, including the practice of yoga meditation, began to develop strongly from this period.

Siddhartha Gautama, the Buddha, introduced to the practice of Hindu meditation a new method or attitude that became prescient. Although protected all his young life he came to realize that life is endless suffering and sought to find a solution to this problem. For six years he followed the yoga method but could make make no progress toward his goal. For a short while, he took on an extreme ascetic form, but then suddenly veered from this kind of commitment.

Almost like Paul on the road to Damascus, he was given sudden, brilliant illumination. "*He allowed himself to move into a new state of meditation in which he stopped concentrating, stopped seeking. In this state, he found enlightenment and became Buddha.*" (See Peck, p.308)

Buddha affirmed the Hindu view of life as suffering. The central distinguishing feature of Buddhism is that there is a middle path between the two extremes of allowing our passions free reign or the practice of extreme asceticism:

"*There is a middle path, avoiding these two extremes... A path which opens the eyes, and bestows understanding, which leads to peace of mind, to the higher wisdom, to full enlightenment, to Nirvana.*" (See Starr, p. 171.

Buddhism is a moderate way. (It would be interesting to compare Buddhist moderation with ancient Athenian emphasis on moderation.) Buddha apparently gave no attention to religious devotion. He upheld the major Hindu doctrines. Love and peace and kindness are concepts abundantly declared in the Buddha's teachings. Hindu and Buddhist agree that if a man is consumed with the things of this world he cannot expect to find union with God.

The Buddha lived 500 years before Jesus Christ. Jesus had a unique and profound relationship with God the Father, Whom He called Abba. Buddha did not claim such a relationship, for he did not concur that spiritual devotion was of any value. He did not believe in miracles, yet the Buddhist tradition is replete with miracles he allegedly performed, such as dropping a toothpick which immediately sprang up as a tree. (See Durant, p.436.)

One could argue that this is just legend, but the same argument could be made of Jesus walking on water.

HERE AN UNDERSTANDING OF MYTH IS VERY IMPORTANT: Myth is not simply imaginary events, but an account of origins or foundations that explain how the world came to be.

Buddha is not divine, but he is splendid none the less. He brought to the world a system of thought and way of life based on love and peace which was as original, if not so sublime, as the message and example of Jesus Christ. (I have wondered how much knowledge Jesus had of the life of Buddha.)

The early Buddhists saluted each other with the phrase, *"peace to all beings."* This is similar to the Hebrew phrase, *"shalom aleichem."* And to the Christian blessing, *"peace and grace from God be unto you."*

****

Chapter VII
The Case For God-Given Universal Values

(with reference to the Philosophy of Immanuel Kant)

During my time as College President, I found and strongly agreed with Alan Bloom's *The Closing of the American Mind (1987)*:

"There is one thing a professor can be absolutely certain of: almost every student entering the University believes that truth is relative. If this belief is put to the test, one can count on the student reaction as uncomprehending. That anyone should regard the proposition as not self-evident astonishes them... the relativity of truth is not a theoretical insight but a moral postulate, the condition of a free society, or so they see it. They have all been equipped with this framework early on, and <u>it is the modern replacement for the unalienable natural rights that used to be the traditional grounds for a free society.</u>"(Alan Bloom)

My interpretation of God's truth is that, while *freedom and justice and democracy* may be sociologically relative, they are also categories of thought which are universally born and working their way to expression in all societies. More fundamentally, these ideals are related to the immanence of dignity and desire for integrity in all people everywhere.Even criminals will havej these traits.

Dignity is personal. The concept of integrity may be applied to an organization and the state as well as to an individual; integrity is the driving desire for authenticity and wholeness. A man's or

woman's dignity, on the other hand refers to the uniqueness of personality and his/her reliance upon it.

Can we believe in these values because we know that they are true for all people everywhere, so that they do not depend on exhortation or dialectical thinking, so that they are not merely the image of good politics? How can this notion of universality be validated? What sources may we depend upon?

While undertaking this exploration, I want to acknowledge that I am trying to work within a paradigm or worldview which may be characterized as empirical/rationalist. My personal beliefs and insights do not accord entirely with this view even though I recognize the "rules of the game."

I believe that the questions of God's grace, love, intervention, transcendence and immanence cannot be approached in this worldview, yet culturally these remain our most powerful and poignant concepts.

In proceeding with this argument, I am following the advice I used to give to students: *"An old English town had three walls around it. In each wall there was a gate. Above the first gate was an inscription, Be bold! Above the second gate, Be bold! Above the third gate, Be not too bold!"*

In the pursuit of truth, we must be bold! When we come to matters of commitment, we must also keep some self doubt and room for critical reflection. In the end, however, it is important to make commitments because our salvation depends upon it.

In his essay on Education, Immanuel Kant said," *Providence has willed, that man shall bring forth for himself the good that lies hidden in his nature, and has spoken, as it were, thus to man: 'Go forth into the world. I have equipped thee with every tendency towards the good. Thy part let it be to develop these tendencies!'"*

The complexity and at times obscurity in Kant's philosophical writings is revealed, however, by the attention he also gives to the depravity of human nature. Especially in his work, *Religion Within the Limits of Reason Alone, he recognizes man's propensity to evil as a result of free will, which, for Kant, is a rational power.*

The conflict of inclinations toward good and evil is described, in part, by such references *as "perversity of the heart" or "a certain insidiousness of the human heart which deceives itself in regard to its own good and evil intentions."..If man/woman is to be held responsible for their corruption, it must be on the grounds of original predisposition to good, from which they have freely departed."*

Since freedom is a "mere idea", it cannot be illustrated in the laws of nature. Therefore it cannot be explained; it can only be defended. Freedom exists, Kant contends, because humans have the power of reason. It is through the rational development of their natural tendencies towards the good that men and women earn their freedom and become worthy of happiness.

Obviously, good will can be subverted, but in Kantian terms, the hope of revival is not lost because man has moral consciousness – – "the moral law within" given by God.

Intrinsic values cannot be described in the social order; they are postulated through moral reasoning. It is the reasoning that counts toward freedom and integrity. In Kant's view, right actions are not sufficient. It is not that right actions have no moral worth, but that only actions taken in knowledge and understanding lead to ethical conduct. In ethical matters, man/woman ought to choose virtue not merely from inclination, but from duty which is defined by Kant as,*" the necessity of an action resulting from respect for* the *law."* The law may be juridical or moral.

A man or woman is ethical in the performance of their duty, in other words, not because they perform certain actions but because they know they oiught to perform them. It is in this sense that we may speak of a <u>person's integrity.</u>

Kant's moral writings lead ultimately to the question of Human relationship to God. In all matters of morality, it is not what God forbids that shines through: God desires not the good but that man/woman <u>choose the good.</u>

In the Kantian system, the idea of God is a heuristic concept: pure reason neither can prove nor disprove God's existence; rather it is a "postulate of practical reason." In other words, reason cannot be extended to an explanation of the spiritual world,the world which transcends experience. However, the will is greater than reason. Free will and moral consciousness lead to belief in God.

Kant helps to remind us that moral philosophy has wrestled with the problem of values longer than has modern social science. The social sciences laid the foundations for cultural relativism.

In all living systems, whether the system is a simple one taken from nature or highly complex, like man, values are built into the system's existence, and there is a norm expressed by all systems and their constant adaptation to their environments. History since the Enlightenment has taught us the weakness of rationalism in that it did not fully understand human nature.

Science lacks the fullness of spiritual insight that artists and mystics and people of faith often display: They may recognize the separateness and miraculousness of a spiritual reality by which men/women, tapping into it, may be genuinely lifted out of alienation and transformed. There is also an individualistic propensity of men/women to risk greatly, sometimes even death, for what is not survival nor escape from evil but spiritual achievement through that "primal and universal psychic energy" existing of itself. (See the works of Teilhard de Chardin.)

"Some day, after we have mastered the winds, the waves, the tides, and gravity, we shall harness for God the energies of love: and then for the second time in the history of the world... Man will have discovered fire."(Teilhard)

If God is not love, the cosmic experiment with the rational animal may be much briefer than the dinosaurs. In that case the purpose of creation is either absent or doesn't matter. But the trends of evolution and human thought seem to support the opposite conclusion: Evolution and thought may be incoherent, but they are as purposeful as arrows aimed at a target.

Therefore, what all men and women think, what commitments they make, and how and why they relate to their Creator are supremely important. The human condition may be such that humans cannot escape suffering and alienation and ultimate destruction except as they finally find a loving God.

****

Chapter VIII
Finding the Christian Tradition

<u>Christ is alive!</u> But Christianity is defensive in a technology-intensive, materialist civilization which has origins in the church but now runs to a scientific cadence. The dominant mode of thought today is not Christian, it is secularist. Belief and unbelief are equally tolerated. Religion is strictly a personal matter. In this state of affairs, Christianity will not be revived by medieval concepts and dogma. Nor will any narrow fundamentalism in service of a proselytizing mission move the church out of a defensive posture. Science simply will not be gunned down, largely because it reports God's truth.

But science is only one way of knowing. It seems clear enough that science based on empirical – rationalist method has definite limits. "New science" comes much closer to poetry and religious insight; there is a merger. In what sense do "quarks" in physics exist? Does it tell us more than Rilke's poetry because poetry does tnot know that the elementary particles of the universe can only be explained by inference?

"We've never, no, not for a single day, pure space before us, such as that which flowers endlessly open into the always world, and never nowhere without no: that pure unsuperintended element we breathe, endlessly knows, and never craves." (Rainer Maria Rilke)

It was in the tradition of Holy Spirit moving the church, that metaphysically there is a transformation occurring of Hellenistic thought penetrating to the need for more sophisticated answers. Paul creates the way for Christianity to break out of Judaic confinement, inevitably leading to use of

Greek concepts to explain Jesus Christ as son of God and Savior. The supernatural power of Jesus to perform miracles was explainable within a Judaic context, as was his charismatic effect on people.

Jewish Christians, or Christian Jews, were committed to a personal God who had been seen up close. It required the greater intellectual strength of Greek philosophy, however, to give depth of appreciation to the nature of this God. In working out the answers to the mystery of Jesus as both divine and human, a dialectical process seems to have unfolded. It is easy to understand how, after Paul, the proliferation of cultural acceptance of Jesus Christ created enormous differences of opinion.

At the same time, still facing persecution and a hostile government in Imperial Rome, the church needed unity. Then after the conversion of Constantine and the official establishment of Christianity, the church was even more torn by schisms and heresy. So, obviously the answer did not come smoothly, peacefully or finally. The mysteries remained, even today they remain.

That takes us back to the place where we started, perhaps with one thing added: it is understood that the metaphysical grounds were provided by the Greeks. But it was, then as now, faith in Jesus Christ that drove and compelled the participants in the struggle to build His church.

In the mind's eye one can see those scholars pouring over the Platonic writings to match faith and reason, and one can understand better that it was not just Hellenistic influence on Christian thinking that a true convergence was brought about by faith seeking and illuminating understanding. Those Platonic writings had what the Hasidic Jews called "sparks of divinity."

It is I think in the sense of long tradition that God in evolutionary process may be understood. In the true Christian tradition, God is present in both the natural and social orders; He is not the "cold outsider ." The appearance of His presence is evident in the Old Testament, accounting for Jewish origins of the tradition.

<u>Then comes the Christ event.</u> Let us define it as the coming of Jesus, his ministry while on earth, and the events immediately following his crucifixion, extending to the beginning of the church. The church begins with the response of Jesus's disciples to His resurrection. It builds through the

organizational work of the apostles, especially Peter and Paul, but in the first century we are still looking at a small Jewish sect.

It is truly remarkable how fast Christianity grew, but it is not difficult to understand its rapid growth if one subscribes to the work of the Holy Spirit. It is more difficult to understand if all spiritual sources of power are denied and events are seen historically as just a tenacious undertaking by a few poor and uneducated Jews.

It was the work of Paul, both ministry and theology, which allowed Christianity to become catholic. Considering how strong were the Jewish ties to ritual and their covenant, Paul must have been a genius to see the need for new doctrine and to provide it in such eloquent essential terms. He provides many if not most of the great faith phrases that fill the language of the Christian tradition.

Paul and his lieutenants enriched the Christian canon so that it becomes a constant inspiration to those Hellenized thinkers who follow him. THe historian, Will Durant, wrote: "Paul had found a dream of Jewish eschatology, confined in Judaic law; he had freed and broadened it into a faith that could move the entire world."

Following Paul are the desert fathers and monastic orders, all defenders of the faith within the church hierarchy, By the end of the fourth century the tradition is well-established, which does not mean the end of heresy, but there was clear doctrine affirming the human and divine natures of Jesus Christ.

The classical Christian tradition is reflected in much of the music and art and the best poetry of Western culture. Perhaps this is because the mystical content is best expressed in these forms. If faith and hope and love survive so will the tradition.

I confess that these notes are lacking, perhaps in many ways, but in one way in particular. The description does not contain the most fundamental, prescient absolute of Christianity – God's love.

Biblically, God sent his son, Jesus Christ, to save us from our sins. I believe a stronger and truer blessing is that Jesus died on the cross for love. It is this universal psychic power expressed in Christianity that distinguishes it from all other world religions.

That is why the tradition shall remain vital even as it finds new interpretation of its sources and new reconciliation with other ways of reaching for the realities of existence. If this is so. the question arises how important is it to understand the historical formulation of Christianity? Does it make any difference whether or not the late Christian recognizes paradox in his or her beliefs?

To put a Christian light on our culture as Paul and his contemporaries attempted to do on theirs, we must understand in depth those things we believe. Otherwise we may fall into the trap Augustine warned about of taking signs for the reality, or of allowing statutes and formulas to become mechanical tools which are the " ankle chains of a continuous immaturity."

I know two scientists, one young and vigorous, the other older and perhaps more stodgy. Both are good Christians. The younger already has an impressive record in his field of biotechnology. He is a thoroughly competent laboratory scientist, much sought after. He does not believe in the theory of evolution.

The other is not well published, but he has had a long and successful teaching career in physics. He is a strict fundamentalist in his approach.

Is it important that they know how the creed they have adopted came to be? Would they care.? I doubt it: their religion is of the heart, not of the mind, their focuses on the saving and healing power of Jesus Christ. They would I believe subscribe to this view.

I disagree with both on some aspects of salvation, but I do not argue with either of them. In His majesty, I believe God prefers that we whisper results to our neighbors.

There is a spiritual realm, a hair breath away every moment we live in this world, and we are as dead as we're going to get unless our souls sail into nothingness – not death but annihilation: – – eternally separated from God. This spiritual world we cannot probe with science, as we do the material world,

Radiant with love that intervenes in our lives sometimes by His grace, I believe it is the cosmic consciousness that is flooding the universe.

****

JOH Cursom Perficio

Theology End Notes

"We shall not cease from exploring, and the end of all our exploration will be to arrive where we started and know the place for the first time." (T.S.Eliot)

Translations of Sacred Texts:

Holy Bible, New King James Version, Copyright 1982 by Thomas Nelson Inc.

Holy Bible, Thompson's Chain Reference Edition

A Sourcebook in Indian Philosophy, Princeton University Press, 1957

George S. Duncan, *The Epistles of Paul to the Galatians, Harper and Brothers, 1934*

Donald Guthrie, *The New Century Bible Commentary: Galatians*, WB Eerdsmans, 1973

****

Secondary Sources:

Jose Ortega y Gasset, *History as a System,* Norton,1961

William James, *The Varities of Religious Experience:A Study in Human Nature, Lectures delivered at Edinburgh*, 1901 – 1902

Robert Nisbet, *The Quest for Community, Oxford University Press, 1953*

Max Weber, *Bureaucracy,* 1922

John B. Moss, *Man's Religions, Revised Edition*, McMillan, 1956

William E. Paden, *Religious Worlds: The Comparative Study of Religion, Beacon* Press, 1988

Will Durant, *Our Oriental Heritage*, Simon & Schuster, 1965

Chester G. Starr, *A History of the Ancient World, Oxford* University Press,1965

John Stott, *The Cross of Christ, Inter-Varsity Press, 1986*

Marcus Borg, *Jesus: A New Vision, Harper and Row, 1987*

Thomas H. Tobin, *The Spirituality of Paul,*Liturgical Press, 1987

Immanuel Kant, *Religion Within Limits of Reason, in* <u>*The Philosophy of Kant*</u>, ed. Carl J. Friedrich, Random House, 1949

Vine's Expository Dictionary of New Testament Words, Hendrickson's Publishers

Immanuel Kant, *Education, University of Michigan, 1960*

George T. Lock Land, *Grow Or Die: The Unifying Principle of Transsformation*, Random House, 1973

Ernest Becker, *The Structure of Evil*, Free Press, 1968

Ervin Laszlo, *Introduction to Systems Philosophy, Gordon and Breach, 1972*

Abraham H. Maslow, *Toward a Psychology of Being, 3rd Edition, Wiley, 1998*

M. Scott Peck, *The Road Less Traveled, Simon & Schuster, 1978*

Charles F. Marden and Gladys Meyer, *Minorities in American Society,* 2nd Edition, American Book Company, 1962

The Autobiography of Malcolm X, 1963

I. F. Stone, *The Pilgrimage of Malcolm X, New York Review, November 11, 1965*

Thomas Wolfe, *You Can't Go Home Again,* Harper, 1940

John O. Hunter, Commentary on Martin Luther King, Jr. in <u>Striving to Be a *College President,*</u> IUniverse, 2011. Also in <u>*For the Love of Poetry,*</u> *2009 and 2013*

****

A Personal Note

During my college presidencies in the late 80s and 90s, my avocation involved study in philosophy and religion. I am immensely grateful for my time spent at St. Bonaventure University, where I enrolled in theology courses; at Oxford University where I participated in the Oxford Round Table and enjoyed a summer on the Thames River; at Harvard University, where I spent my leave of absence; and at the Abbey of Genesee, where through many retreats, I became introduced to monastic life, and found the wonderful tapes of Thomas Merton, Novice Master at Gethseme Abbey, Kentucky.

These institutions provided for me not only rich sources for academic study, but they were wonderful places of peace and spiritual contemplation. For the most part, I have been a lone ranger in my searches but I am deeply indebted to many sources, such as those itemized above, and for the galvanizing opportunities on my long, sometimes erratic road to conversion. I thank God for His blessings on this road-- for His lovingkindness, healing power, and forgiveness.

Any errors or mistakes in this book are mine alone. JOH

Cursom Perficio

Sir William Hunter of Hunterstone, 13th century

Jane Robertson Hunter

Celtic Church, Iona, Scotland

Hunter Clan Motto

Dr. John O. Hunter

Printed in the United States
By Bookmasters